INDIA

AN ILLUSTRATED HISTORY

ILLUSTRATED HISTORIES FROM HIPPOCRENE

Arizona
The Celtic World
China
Cracow
Egypt
England
France
Greece
Ireland
Israel
Italy
Korea
London
Mexico
Moscow
Paris
Poland
Poland in World War II
Romania
Russia
Sicily
Spain
Tikal
Vietnam
Wales

INDIA

AN ILLUSTRATED HISTORY

Prem Kishore and
Anuradha Kishore Ganpati

HIPPOCRENE BOOKS, INC.
New York

Photographs on pages 65, 72, 97, 158, 164, 181, 189, 193, 199, 201, 210 courtesy of the Government of India Department of Tourism.

ISBN 0-7818-0944-4

For information, address:
    Hippocrene Books, Inc.
    171 Madison Avenue
    New York, NY 10016

Cataloging-in-Publication data available from the Library of Congress.

Printed in the United States of America.

Acknowledgments

It was a special privilege to work with Hippocrene Books, which gave us this wonderful opportunity and trusted us with this commitment. We are grateful to Anne Kemper, our editor, for her superb expertise, perception, insight, and delightful humor and for disciplining us when we were intoxicated with overblown metaphors and assumptions.

We thank our dear friend, author Robert Arnett, for the excellent photographs he shared so generously and for his inspiring book *India Unveiled.*

We thank the Government of India's Department of Tourism for invitations to many regions in India over the years.

Dr. Anantha Nageswaran, Director of Credit Suisse Private Banking, contributed the political and economic analysis in Chapter 12, "India Today." His skilful analysis of facts and statistics provides an enlightening perspective on modern India.

Our gratitude goes out to the anchor in our lives, husband/ father Prem Kishore Gambeer, for his wisdom, enthusiasm, lucid thinking, and constant encouragement. Nasir and Sangeetha in Switzerland contributed their support and abiding faith in our work.

Thanks to Chetan for his balanced overview, as well as his extraordinary patience in compiling photographs and rescuing lost computer files.

The stories of India are a special gift to Aneek, Aleena, Taha, and Uddanta. May this book help them and all readers to discover the enthralling history and culture of India.

Contents

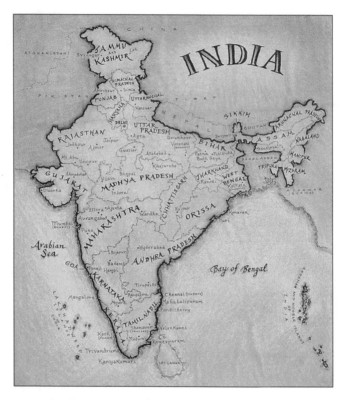

Map of India (courtesy of Robert Arnett, India Unveiled*).*

Preface

India is daunting, bewildering, and unique. It is a country that defies easy characterization and embodies stunning opposites: the ancient and the new, rich and poor, sensual and ascetic, secular and spiritual. India is a nuclear power, and yet astrologers still decide the auspicious time for sanctifying a marriage or starting a business. If there is a collision between the past and the present in India, there also has been an astonishing continuity and development of culture over the last 4,500 years.

For us, the process of learning about India while writing this book was an adventure in itself. We had the formidable task of bringing together the many works on this subject to create a concise account. As we explored the history and heritage of India, we decided not to provide a mere catalog of facts and dates, but chose to share many of the moving, dramatic, and varied myths and legends that we discovered.

Part I (chapters 1–12) of this book provides a brief overview of India's political and economic history, from 2500 BCE to the present. Part II (chapters 13–17) describes the nation's culture, including religion, customs and rituals, the arts, and cuisine.

Many scholars have interpreted the history of India and their writings have made a significant impact on our work. This is not a book for the specialist/researcher in Indian history. It is a lively introduction to this country's history, people, politics, and culture. We hope our account provokes the reader's curiosity and desire to learn more.

PART I

DISCOVERING INDIA

― 1 ―
The Indus Valley Civilization
(2500 BCE–1600 BCE)

THE BRICK STORY

Life in earliest India was uncovered beginning with a few bricks.

1850 While constructing a steel railway line between Karachi and Punjab, British engineers stumbled on a few shapeless mounds and kiln-baked bricks. Lacking in curiosity, but practical-minded, they used the scattered bricks as ballast for their railway track (which finally traversed 25,000 miles across India).

1853 Sir Alexander Cunningham, an amateur archaeologist and general in the British army, was intrigued by vague rumors and stories of the brick finds. He initiated an investigation of the site of the railway tracks and extricated numerous antiquities, including several seals and examples of pictographic script. While he suspected the enormity of his find, he was unable to decipher the inscriptions.

1921 Britain's new director general of archaeology in India, Sir John Marshall, learned of the finds and assembled a team headed by Rakhal Das Banerji to launch an extensive excavation. This expedition uncovered the buried remains of one of the world's oldest and richest civilizations.

The discovery of a few bricks led to the unearthing of the vanished cities of Mohenjodaro and Harappa, some four hundred miles apart. Here, an urban and sophisticated Indus culture, named after the life-giving Indus River, flourished around 2500 BCE.

This extraordinary chapter in world history, which had been hitherto unknown, is now transforming our understanding of ancient India. A profile emerges of an ethnic composition of perhaps five groups. The earliest was the Negrito, followed by proto-Australoid, Mongoloid, Alpine, and Mediterranean. There are several sites in India and Pakistan where the early dwellers lived. Caves in the hillsides of Madhya Pradesh and Bhimbetka in India are littered with remnants of their stone tools and flints. Another exciting recent analysis of inscriptions in Harappa and Mohenjodaro have led scholars to believe that they could be related to the Dravidian language, spoken by the Dravidians who entered India before 2000 BCE, passing through Iran, Mesopotamia, and Baluchistan. Some historians connect the Dravidian language with even ancient Egypt and Nubian languages. The Dravidian language is now subdivided into four major languages in South India, Tamil, Telugu, Malayalam and Kannada and is spoken by nearly 200 million people.

THE CITIES OF MOHENJODARO AND HARAPPA

Archaeologists have found the Indus Valley cities of Mohenjo-daro and Harappa to be masterpieces of urban planning. Functional and utilitarian architecture, small stone statues, and large granaries reflect the sophistication and development of these communities, which may have had as many as thirty thousand residents in each city. The city streets were laid at right angles in a rigidly mathematical grid pattern, with avenues running north and south, as well as east and west. Indoor baths and toilets were connected by an elaborate system of drains and water chutes to sewers running under the main streets. Perhaps due to the people's fear of pollution and their need for ritual cleansing, hundreds of drains were built, and the cities also featured a highly advanced system of garbage collection.

The people lived in houses made from fired brick. These ranged from small huts to mansions that were often two or more stories high. The types of houses clearly delineated the upper and lower strata of society and reflected a hierarchy of class, perhaps serving as the forerunner of the more complex caste system that surfaced later. Public buildings, including the vast granaries for the storage of surplus wheat and barley, reveal the crops, farming techniques, and building skills of the people. The most famous of these buildings is the Great Bath at Mohenjodaro, an oblong bathing area thirty-nine feet in length, twenty-two feet in width, and eight feet deep.

Farming, trading, and shipping contributed to the wealth of the two cities. The Indus Valley civilization enjoyed a prosperous trade with its contemporary civilizations, Egypt and Mesopotamia, both by land and by sea. Grain was exported in large quantities, along with precious stones, pearls, and different kinds of wood. A fragment of dyed cotton has been found at Mohenjodaro, indicating the use of cotton for clothing. Copper, bronze, lead, tin, and remnants of furnaces provide further evidence of a wealthy, sophisticated society.

Additional finds—including household utensils, painted pottery, dice, chessmen, coins, stone carvings, gold and silver bangles, ear ornaments, and necklaces—continue to amaze archaeologists. Other fascinating discoveries include a bronze statue of a dancing girl, as well as terra-cotta toy carts and animals. More than one thousand soapstone seals have been found; they feature exquisitely carved figures of horned bulls, elephants, tigers, and antelopes above pictographic inscriptions that have not yet been deciphered but provide examples of a written language. A female figure depicted as a horned Goddess (perhaps the Mother Goddess who presided over fertility and birth) was discovered on seals and amulets. Another seal depicts a three-horned deity standing in the middle of a tree, while a figure outside the tree appears to be worshipping it as a tree God. The bull appears to be another recurring motif on the seals; some associate it with the sacred bull Nandi, Lord Shiva's mount in Hindu tradition.

When bodies were buried in brick chambers, their heads pointed north. The skeletons were richly ornamented and placed in coffins. A number of pots were buried alongside them. Graves reveal skeletons of couples, which may presage sati (suttee), the Hindu custom in which the widow follows her husband to the funeral pyre and beyond.

The Indus Valley civilization appears to have disappeared as suddenly as it was discovered. No one is sure about what happened: the demise of this great civilization could have been caused by invading tribes, perhaps the Aryans; there may have been a ravaging drought, caused by the expansion of the neighboring desert, or a deluge when the Indus River changed its course. There was a gradual disappearance of the Indus sites, with the crumbling of buildings, smaller homes built on higher ground due to heavy flooding and chaos resulting in the decline of Harappan culture by 1700 BCE. By 1650 BCE, the cities were abandoned and the people vanished.

Female figurine with three chokers and necklace from Harappa (copyright George Helmes/Harappa Archaeological Research Project, courtesy Dept of Archaeology and Museums, Govt of Pakistan).

Today, radiocarbon chronologies and satellite imaging are closing the gaps in history revealing the Indus Valley civilization's trade routes by land and sea with Mesopotamia and Sumeria. Other cities recently have been discovered in the northwest of India by the banks of the now-dry Saraswati River. Excavations of this ancient riverbed continue to this day. Instead of the old theory that development of the Indus Valley civilization stemmed from that of ancient Greece, discoveries and attempts are now being made to prove that Indian civilization has to be studied on its own merits. Historians are incorporating new evidence from archaeology and an analytical study of society, which has resulted in comparative studies. In any case, it is certain that the Indus Valley civilization burst into history as a stunning, brilliant meteor. And then vanished.

— 2 —
The Vedic Age: The Aryans and Alexander the Great
(1500 BCE–322 BCE)

Was there an Aryan Invasion that brought "civilization" to India? Debate and speculation surround the questions of whether there was an invasion by the Aryans and whether civilization in India preceded or followed them. Proponents of the invasion theory insist that tall, fair-haired, and light-skinned Aryans fled from their homelands in Central Asia, somewhere between the Caspian and the Black Seas, perhaps the steppes of central and southern Russia. Some tribes went west to England and Ireland, while other tribes invaded Europe, Greece, and Germany. Others moved east to Iran and Anatolia now called Turkey. Drought, famine, or floods may have been the causes of the migrations. The Aryans entered India around 1500 BCE, through the Hindu Kush Mountains in northwest India and conquered the "primitive," indigenous dark-skinned people, introducing religion, the classical language of Sanskrit, architecture, and civilization in general.

Recent investigative scholarship contests the hypothesis of an Aryan invasion, proposing that the marauding nomadic Aryan invaders encountered a flourishing civilization that was already in existence. These scholars argue that the indigenous Indus people had already reached a remarkable level of communal living and architectural ability long before the invasion of the Aryans. They also remind us that the word *arya* means "noble, highborn," referring to a characteristic and not a race.

Aryan culture ultimately outlasted that of the Indus Valley civilization and laid the foundations of Hinduism. The supposedly "superior" culture and lifestyle that the Aryans brought to India included a language, Sanskrit, which philologists found similar to the classical languages of Europe: Greek, Latin, and German. (Sanskrit means "pure, perfect, sacred.") However, the Aryans used no writing system.

Historical scholarship and comparative studies about the Aryans come from archaeological evidence and Vedic literature composed during this period. It is believed that Aryans rode in chariots (some contest this because nomads generally do not travel in chariots), fought with spears, loved gambling, and drank *soma*, an intoxicating drink consumed at religious rituals.[1]

The Aryans depended on their herds of cattle, which provided food, clothing, and transport. Marriage was forbidden outside the group for fear of dilution of the racial identity. Cooking became a religious ritual, with food being offered to the Gods. The father was the head of the household, and when the father died the eldest son was required to perform the rituals. The son's presence was essential at important ceremonies. This custom is still prevalent in Hindu society. The Aryans had a great love of music and song and constantly chanted and sang hymns; however, some astronomical references in the Rig-Veda allude to the origin of these hymns in a pre-Aryan era.

A tough, nomadic people, the Aryans organized themselves into individual units that spread over northern India and the Deccan. They planted barley, raised cattle, irrigated land, and

1. Soma is the milky fermented liquor from the soma plant (*Sarcostemma intermedium*), a milkweed, that was drunk by priests to obtain immortality. In Hindu mythology, because of its powerful healing qualities, soma was an object of dispute between Gods and demons.

took great interest in handicrafts and guilds. They were painters, sailors, and hunters. They also worked with ivory, bronze, copper, wood, leather, and stone. With trade and travel accelerating between Afghanistan, Persia, Egypt, and Mesopotamia, barter gave way to the use of cattle as currency; later this currency was replaced by heavy copper coinage. A credit system became popular, and gambling with dice became an important part of social life.

The Aryans perceived themselves as a noble, skilled, and courageous people. For the purpose of social and economic organization, society was initially divided into three classes: warriors, priests, and commoners. Gradually, a structure of four main castes or *varnas* ("colors" in Sanskrit) became defined.

In one theory, the four varnas were created from the various parts of Brahma, the creator. The Brahmins, or priests, created from Brahma's mouth, did all the religious work. Gradually, the Brahmins became the dominant, privileged, hereditary caste, wielding tremendous power and control, even over the king. Next came the Kshatriyas (kings, warriors), created from the hands of Brahma. Their duty was to fight until death. At the third level, the Vaishyas, created from Brahma's thighs, were merchants, traders, and artisans. They were followed by the Shudras, created from his feet, who were farmers. Existing outside of the caste system, the lowest strata of society consisted of the untouchables, whose main occupations were menial chores such as sweeping roads, cleaning lavatories, and cremating the dead. This fifth strata of people was believed to have been the result of encounters between Aryan and non-Aryan communities.

Another theory suggests that human beings were believed to possess one of the following three qualities and to perform occupations based on this quality. The Sattva quality of the

Brahmin expressed knowledge and intelligence; the Rajas quality of the Kshatriyas expressed bravery, while the Tamas quality of the lower classes expressed mediocrity and other negative qualities. Even dietary practice was believed to have been an important factor in this complex structure of classification. The Sattvic diet of the Brahmins comprised vegetables, fruit, and milk; the Rajasic diet of the Kshatriyas included special deer meat, while the Shudras followed a Tamasic diet and ate other kinds of meat.

The Aryans also brought with them a new pantheon of Gods and new religious beliefs that revolved around nature and the environment. Deities were personified by the sky, sun, earth, fire, light, wind, water, and rain. Brahma, the most powerful deity, was the creator of the universe.

The Vedas and the Upanishads

Most of our understanding of the Aryan period and the foundation of Hinduism is derived from the collection of evocative Sanskrit hymns, the four Vedas (meaning Divine Knowledge), believed to have been composed between 1500 and 1000 BCE (or even a thousand years earlier), as well as the two epic poems, the *Mahabharata* and the *Ramayana.* The mystical section of the Vedas comprises Brahmanas, Aranyakas, and the Upanishads.

The Vedas, it is believed, emanated from Brahma's breath and were revealed orally to the *munis,* or sages. Rich in lyricism, rhythm, and eloquence, the Vedas are infused with instructions and ritual observations.

Devotees at temple at Somnathpur (courtesy of Robert Arnett, India Unveiled*).*

The Rig-Veda (Hymns of Praise) is considered to be the original text from which are derived the Sama Veda (knowledge of melody for chanting), Yajur Veda (knowledge of sacrifices and rituals), and Atharva Veda (knowledge of magic formulas, spells, sorcery). Suffused in poetry, the one thousand and twenty-eight hymns of the Rig-Veda praise the Gods and petition for rain, victory in war, a good harvest, healthy herds, and longevity. The supreme deities were Agni (bearing fire), Indra (bearing rain), and Surya (the Sun and the source of heat). Other honored deities included Earth Mother Prithivi; Vayu, the wind; Varuna, the sky; and Usha, dawn, daughter of the sky. Rudra was the tempestuous storm God, and Yama was the God of death. Certain animals were regarded as sacred, particularly the bull, which later became the mount of Shiva. Sacred spirits were believed to dwell in animals, stones, trees, streams, mountains, and stars. Deities included Hanuman the monkey God, Yakshas or tree Gods, and serpents.

The later Vedic Age, which began sometime after 1000 BC, produced the Brahmanas, or instructions for ritual and prayer, which placed every facet of Aryan life under control of the priests. Often there are detailed instructions of elaborate ritual sacrifices, and it was at this time that priests attained a deified status. Cows were used as currency and soon became a symbol of worship. To the Brahmanas were added the Aranyakas ("belonging to the forests"), instructions for religious hermits, and the Upanishads (circa 600 BCE). The Upanishads contain two hundred works in prose and poetry fused with discourses on religion, philosophy, and mysteries of the universe. *Upa* means near and *shad* means "to sit," so *Upanishad* means "sitting near the guru." The Upanishads have been described as comprising a philosophic and intellectual defiance against Brahmanism and the Kshatriya-Brahmin struggle for supremacy. In the Aryan society, officially priests were more powerful than kings, since they propitiated the Gods and dictated a social order. In actuality, significant power struggles often occurred between these groups.

Considered to emanate from the breath of Brahma, the Vedas were meant to be sung and not read. They passed from generation to generation through memorization and recitation. The emphasis was on "utterance" of the prayers. To transcribe these divine revelations onto the evanescent leaf or bark was sacrilegious. Thus religious and literary writing was condemned. According to one couplet in the epic *Mahabharata,* writers were consigned to eternal punishment.[2]

Young priest (courtesy of Robert Arnett, India Unveiled).

The Vedas reveal the manner in which beliefs in this society slowly developed as the Aryans adapted to their new environment, becoming settled. The epic poems, the *Ramayana* and the *Mahabharata,* followed the Rig-Veda. This literature formulates the religion and philosophy of Hinduism, consolidating legends, myth, ritual, and commentary. The

2. Even now, the oral tradition is considered superior to the written in India. Children are taught the *slokas* (prayers) even at the age of two, and are encouraged to memorize and pronounce each syllable with perfection.

epic poems were succeeded much later by the Puranas, "old," stories of ancient times. The eighteen Puranas of about four hundred thousand couplets record the form of Hinduism that prevailed after the Vedic period. They indicate that faith was placed in at least one principal divinity in whom was manifested all things, and who was worshipped in diverse forms. Vishnu and Shiva appear to be dominant.

THE EPIC STORIES

The Heroism of Rama in the Ramayana

Like Homer's *Iliad,* the Indian epics offer a heritage of characters who aspire to be heroic, devout, and pure. Longer than the *Iliad* and the *Odyssey,* the *Ramayana* is the favorite story of millions even today. It is believed to have existed in oral form as early as 1500 BCE but was written down in Sanskrit by the sage Valmiki around 400 BCE, a century before the *Mahabharata.* The *Ramayana* is divided into seven *kandas,* or sections, containing some fifty thousand lines.

It is the story of prince Rama of Ayodhya, heir to the throne of Kosala and seventh incarnation of Lord Vishnu.[3] Rama is the eldest son of Dasaratha in ancient India. The king has three wives. During a battle, the king is gravely wounded, and one of his wives, Kaikeyi, saves his life. In gratitude, he promises her a boon. When Rama, the eldest son and rightful

---

3. Vishnu is the Preserver and the central deity of the Hindu trinity—Brahma, Vishnu, and Shiva. Vishnu's protecting powers have been manifested in a variety of forms, called avatars, in which one or more portions are manifested in the shape of a human being, an animal, or a combination of human and animal. The seventh and eighth avatars of Vishnu are those of Rama and Krishna. All ten avatars correct evil and effect good on Earth.

The cosmic Shiva (courtesy of Robert Arnett, India Unveiled*).*

heir, is about to succeed Dasaratha, Kaikeyi requests her boon, asking the king to banish Rama from the kingdom for fourteen years and to enthrone her son Bharatha. Rama is exiled. His wife Sita and brother Lakshmana follow him and take refuge in the forests. Bharatha refuses the throne and sets off in search of Rama. He finds Rama and urges him to return to the throne, but Rama is unswerving in his obedience to his father. Bharatha returns to the kingdom and places the wooden sandals worn by Rama on the seat of the throne and rules in his name.

Rama faces the greatest trial of his life in the forest when Ravana, the demon king of Sri Lanka abducts Sita. Rama goes to Sri Lanka and, with the help of the monkey God Hanuman and an army of monkeys, rescues Sita from Ravana. Rama then returns to his kingdom and is crowned. But Sita's innocence in the abduction is under doubt, as she is found pregnant. People gossip that she might have been seduced by Ravana. Sita proves her innocence by walking through fire. The fire God, Agni, returns her to Rama unscathed. Still, rumors persist, and Sita is exiled to the forest, where she gives birth to twin sons, Luv and Kush. She is finally reunited with Rama fifteen years later. Once again, she is asked to prove her innocence. Unable to endure further humiliation, Sita calls on Bhoodevi (Mother Earth) to testify to her innocence. The Earth opens and swallows her up in a symbolic gesture of accepting and embracing her daughter. (The word "sita" means "furrow.")

The faithful and beautiful wife Sita, daughter of King Janaka, is regarded as the ideal Hindu woman who has chosen[4] for her husband Rama the perfect son, husband, and ruler. The

4. Sita chose her husband at a "Swayamvara," a ceremony whereby a Princess selects her suitor in a trial of strength. At the Swayamvara, when no suitor could bend a bow, Rama not only bent the bow but broke it.

18

Ramayana is also a story of dharma, a code of conduct for every person that promotes moral, social, cultural order, stability, and continuity. In addition, the *Ramayana* extols the austere life of a forest home, brotherly love, wifely devotion, commitment to marriage through hardships, and the victory of virtue over evil.

Every year, episodes from the *Ramayana* are enacted all across India at religious festivals, and popular television series depicting the heroic stories of the *Ramayana* captivate Indian audiences even today. Practically every child in India knows the outline of the story and the characters. And almost every young woman wishes to be as virtuous as Sita and to have a husband as heroic as Rama, as well as a brother-in-law like courageous Lakshmana.

As there is no single concept of India, similarly, there is no one version of the *Ramayana* in India. It has been translated into numerous vernacular languages with as many interpretations. For instance, the sixteenth-century poet Tulsidas, an ardent devotee of Rama, was unable to accept the fact that his Lord Rama would subject his wife to so much sorrow. Thus his version, the *Ramcharitmanas* in the language of Hindi, ends with the return of Rama and Sita to Ayodhya after the rescue of Sita. In another version, in the Bengali language, Ravana is a portrayed as a hero. Yet another interpretation indicates that Sita's test by fire was added later to the oral tradition of the *Ramayana.*

The Story of the **Mahabharata**

Divided into eighteen *parvas,* or books, consisting of some two hundred twenty thousand lines, the *Mahabharata* is an epic poem of the Great War and the struggle for the throne between the five Pandava brothers and their one hundred cousins, the Kauravas, at Kurukshetra (a plain near Delhi). It is said that the sage Vyasa dictated the *Mahabharata* to his scribe, the elephant God Ganesha.[5] It is the longest of all the world's epics: four times longer than the *Ramayana* and seven times the length of the *Iliad* and the *Odyssey* together. It is rich in character, legend, and lore.

The story concerns two branches of an ancient royal family. The Kauravas are the progeny of the blind Dhritarashtra, and the Pandavas are the progeny of Dhritarashtra's younger brother, Pandu. The rightful heir to the throne is Dhritarashtra, but because he is blind he is passed over and Pandu becomes king. When Pandu dies at a young age, Dhritarashtra succeeds to the throne, but the cousins carry on a feud over the succession for generations.

In the course of the narrative, the five Pandava brothers marry one woman (Draupadi), lose their kingdom in the throw of the dice, and are banished to the forest for thirteen years. On their return their demands are refused, and a climatic battle is fought between the Pandavas and the Kauravas on the plains of Kurukshetra for eighteen days. The Pandavas win, reclaiming their lost inheritance.

The *Mahabharata* explores courage, as well as human frailty, dynastic struggles, chivalry, hatred, jealousy, faith, and

5. It is said that Vyasa composed the poem in his mind for three years, at the end of which he prayed to Brahma for a scribe. Ganesha was chosen but agreed on one condition: that his tusk (the instrument of writing) would never stop and that Vyasa would never pause in thought. Vyasa countered this challenge by stating that Ganesha should never write something that he did not understand. Thus the *Mahabharata* was committed to writing with great discussion and contemplation between Vyasa and Ganesha.

vice in the form of a dramatic gambling match, where Draupadi is gambled away by Yudhisthira, king of the Pandavas. Draupadi is dragged before the assembled crowd and disrobed of her sari. She calls on Lord Krishna to save her from the terrible ordeal. Krishna responds by making the sari an endless garment, thus saving her honor. Draupadi loosens her hair and vows she will never knot it again until it is washed in the blood of her enemies. Draupadi's honor was finally avenged in the battle between the Pandavas and the Kauravas: she was even present on the fateful eighteenth night when the Pandavas proved victorious.

The Story of the Bhagvad Gita

The kernel of the *Mahabharata* is the *Bhagvad Gita* , the song of the Divine One, a dialogue between Lord Krishna (a manifestation of Vishnu) in human form and the warrior Arjuna, a Pandava, on the battlefield of Kurukshetra some five thousand years ago. This magnificent relationship with the Supreme is illustrated in a powerful discourse on self-realization, religion, ego, duty, the purpose of human existence, materialism, and life after death.

Arjuna is afflicted by self-doubt during the battle of Kurukshetra and discusses the validity and justification of war with his charioteer. Lord Krishna, although related to both warring families, refuses to take any one side and instead serves as the charioteer of Arjuna's war vehicle. During the battle, Krishna reveals himself to Arjuna and offers a philosophical discourse on the nature of the universe, as well as the meaning of duty and the path to the Supreme Being.

This unparalleled dialogue between man (Arjuna) and creator (Krishna) forms the *Bhagvad Gita,* in which the Hindu doctrine is fully explained. A tormented Arjuna cries in anguish at having to kill his kinsmen in battle. Krishna replies that a Spirit exists that is everlasting.

Containing eighteen chapters and seven hundred verses, the *Bhagvad Gita* is a message from God to a distraught humanity and a powerful influence on Hindu thought and philosophy. Freedom from action driven by desire is central to the theme of the *Bhagvad Gita.* It advises detachment from the external world, which is *maya,* an illusion, because it is inconstant, forever changing, and hence cannot be the truth. The ultimate reality is within us, and to seek it is to seek peace and bliss.

JAINISM, BUDDHISM, AND BHAKTI

Vedic ritual, Brahmin supremacy, and the caste system soon fostered discontent among the common people, who found expression in two alternate religious philosophies: Jainism and Buddhism.

Jainism

Jainism was founded by Vardhamana Mahavira, a prince turned sage, around 500 BCE in western Bengal. He was the twenty-fourth and last of the Jain prophets known as *tirthankars,* or finders of the path. He rebelled against the Hindu belief in caste.

A Kshatriya by birth, Mahavira left his wealth behind, renounced the world, divested himself of clothing, and wandered

Large sculpture of Jain tirthankars carved at Gwalior fort (courtesy of Robert Arnett, India Unveiled*).*

Lord Bahubali Gomateshwara, first Jain tirthankar (prophet)
(courtesy of Robert Arnett, India Unveiled*).*

as an ascetic in pursuit of spiritual truth and understanding. He condemned the caste system, organized a celibate clergy, preached ahimsa (or nonviolence), austerity, tolerance, and self-discipline. After thirteen years of sacrifice and denial, he was given the title of "*Jina*," conqueror of worldly passions. *Jaina* means "follower of Jina."

The ideal Jain believes that the universe is infinite and not created by a deity. Jains believe in reincarnation and eventual *moksha,* spiritual salvation, as well as reverence for all life. Mahavira taught that abstinence from injury to any living thing was the secret of happiness and release from the mundane world. Traditionally, Jains do not eat honey (regarding it as the life of a bee); they strain water to destroy the microorganisms, veil their mouths lest they destroy microbes in the atmosphere, screen their lamps to protect insects, and sweep the ground before treading on it in case their foot should trample a living thing, like an ant. Many Jains renounce the world (including sexuality) in search of ultimate happiness. Today there are two sects: the Shwetambara, who wear white robes, and the Digambara (sky clad), who renounce all clothing as a sign of their detachment from material possessions.

Jainism was predominantly confined to India as the extreme asceticism had limited appeal. It was not possible for Jains to practice agriculture and crafts, since this endangered the life of other creatures, and so Jains became moneylenders, financiers, and traders.

Buddhism and Siddhartha Gautama

In the city of Kapilavastu, on the night of the full Moon, Queen Maya of the Shakya clan garlanded and perfumed herself before falling into a deep sleep. She dreamed that four great kings took her to the Himalayas, and their queens anointed her with oils and laid her on a bed in a golden mansion. There, she dreamed of a white elephant circling her. It appeared to enter her womb. The queen related the dream to the king, who asked for its interpretation from sixty-four Brahmins. They told him that the queen had conceived a son who would become a Buddha, a remover of ignorance. At the end of ten months, in 563 BCE, Queen Maya went to a grove of sal trees, took hold of a branch, and delivered the baby. This is just one of the legends of the birth of Siddhartha Gautama, the Buddha.

Born a Kshatriya, Siddhartha was the son of a chieftain king in the foothills of the Himalayas. At the age of twenty-nine, Siddhartha was driving his chariot and enjoying the beauty of the countryside when he confronted an old man, a very sick man, and a corpse being carried to the cremation ghats. These sights disturbed him profoundly and raised questions about pain, death, and mortality. Troubled and ashamed of his selfish life of splendor and riches, he resolved to become an ascetic. Leaving his palace, wife, and son, he wandered in the forests for six years. He was repelled by his society's trappings of inherited piety, ritual, and wealth and went in pursuit of principles that the Upanishads expounded. According to the Upanishads, man had to atone for evil and constantly was reborn, depending on his karma. Karma is the belief that your good and evil actions in one life will determine the circumstances of your next life. Siddartha realized that if a man could live a just life, showing love, patience, and compassion to all, he would be spared the cycle of perpetual rebirth. It was through the idea of "self" and selfishness that men are vulnerable to birth, aging, illness, and death.

Siddartha urged people to lay aside the sword and not to place importance on ritualistic customs. His followers were tired of the greedy and manipulative priests who insisted that one secured sacroscant powers by virtue of birth alone. These preachings were more universal in appeal than the more severe asceticism of Jainism.

After he achieved enlightenment, Siddhartha was addressed as Buddha (the Enlightened One). Buddha taught through conversations, parables, and stories, much like Jesus and Socrates. Accompanied by his disciples, he wandered from town to town, meditating in the day and discoursing at night.

Buddha promoted the Four Noble Truths:

1. In all of life there is suffering.
2. All human suffering comes from desire and attachment to transient things.
3. To cease suffering, we must end our desire and attachment.
4. To eliminate desire and attachment, we must pursue righteous behavior and attitude.

According to Buddha, wisdom lay in stilling all desire. Nirvana (bliss following one's release from the cycle of reincarnation) came from the removal of selfish desire, and the reward of the highest saintliness was never to be reborn. This religious philosophy ultimately was spread by Buddhist monks south to Sri Lanka and northeast to China, Japan, Korea, and the whole of Southeast Asia.

Buddha died at the age of eighty. After his death, Buddhism went through two thousand years of transition. Two centuries after Buddha's death, Ashoka, the third Mauryan king, became a Buddhist. By the latter part of the third century BCE, the order had split into different factions and Buddhism

Standing Buddha caves, Ajanta (courtesy of Robert Arnett, India Unveiled).

had begun its slow decline in India. Today it is significant mainly in the areas of its origins. It was easily marginalized as the followers were a minority. During the Moghul rule, Hinduism was already an integral part of the lives of people so it survived. But Buddhism had already spread to Nepal, Tibet, China, Japan, and Korea, and other parts of Southeast Asia, flourishing as people were attracted to the rationality of its teachings. Religious contact and trade led to the exchange of ideas and artistic traditions in these regions. Today, monks and monasteries remain the focal point of Buddhism, which still emphasizes meditation, nonviolence, moral law, charity, and moderation.

Comparison of Jainism and Buddhism and the Rise of Bhakti

There was much in common between Jainism and Buddhism. Both of these independent faiths emerged as a serious challenge to Brahmin orthodoxy and were advocated by Kshatriya men who were not Brahmin by birth. Both religions grew out of Hinduism and rejected the authority of the Vedas, as well as ritual and Brahminism; and both emphasized nonviolence and tolerance. The philosophy was not complex, but simple and practical and preached in commonly spoken languages in Magadha, South Bihar, and neighboring districts. The disintegration of both these religions was gradual and spread over many centuries. The Brahmins never lost their hold over India, however, and in the following Gupta period there was a powerful Hindu or Brahminic revival. Hinduism triumphed throughout the length and breadth of India.

In the sixth and seventh centuries (500–750 CE) a similar response to Brahminism emerged in the Bhakti movement, which was formed by reformist leaders and supporters with preference for the lower-caste communities. Different schools emerged around poets and gurus who often used song and dance in worship. The most popular Hindu deities worshipped were Rama and Krishna. Bhakti cults devoted to Lord Shiva and Goddess Shakti are also popular. This movement embraced the low-caste and outcaste Hindus, and worship came in many simple forms. Deities could be made of clay or mud, and bananas, flowers, coconuts, and fruits could be offered by devotees even at a wayside shrine, not necessarily in a temple. Sant Tukaram of Maharashtra and the sixteenth-century Rajput Princess Mira Bai epitomized the passion that characterized this movement.

THE MAGADHAN STATE

There began a comfortable economic prosperity with the expansion of trade. Monasteries and nunneries were built as the exchange of new, reformist ideas occurred. Artisans were organized into guilds, with each guild inhabiting a particular section of town. Trade routes extended from the Ganges delta to the Burma coast. The use of a commercial script for trade was becoming popular. Also during this time, classical Sanskrit was becoming the language of the Brahmins and the learned and was used during Vedic ceremonies. Other popular forms of Sanskrit—Prakrit and Pali—also were used. Hindustani, a vernacular, became the language of the northern part of India, while the Deccan kept its old Dravidian languages: Tamil, Telugu, Kannada, and Malayalam.

A number of kingdoms are documented in the Buddhist texts of the Vedic period. Because kingship that emerged from the Kshatriya class had become hereditary and vested with divinity, there were elaborate rituals and sacrifices associated with it. Chief among them was the Ashwamedha Yagna, in which a special horse wandered across the country, with the king claiming all of the territory that the horse covered. The kingdom of Magadha became the wealthiest and most important. Its villages were headed by local chiefs, and the administration was divided into executive, judicial, and military functions.

Bimbisara (lived ca. 550–491 BCE) ruled Magadha with great political acumen. He was a great supporter of both Jainism and Buddhism. It is said that Bimbisara was so impressed by Buddha that he offered him half his kingdom. The flourishing capital of Magadha, Rajgir (abode of the kings), was a spiritual center for scholars and philosophers. The son of Bimbisara was Ajatashatru (ruled 491–461 BCE), who murdered his father and ascended the throne. He was succeeded by five kings, all of whom had short-lived dynasties, ending in 321 BCE.

In the sixth century BCE, the wealthy and powerful state of Magadha in North India extended across the eastern Gangetic plain now known as Bihar and Orissa. Legends of its glory, opulence, and splendor reached Alexander the Great, king of Macedon, Greece, the master of the Mediterranean world.

India had already come into contact with Greece when Cyrus the Great of Persia (558–535 BCE) conquered the Greek cities of Asia Minor. His successor, Darius, annexed Sindh and Punjab in 518 BCE. Tiring of bloody campaigns, many of his soldiers settled down in India and formed small settlements. Traders, explorers, and adventurers also found themselves lured to India. Travelers returning to their homelands told of gold dust guarded by gigantic ants that were smaller than dogs and larger than foxes, and of Indians mounted on swift camels who plundered the gold at midday when the ants were asleep in their holes. In addition to the exotic and bizarre legends of travelers, significant influences flowed from India to Greece. Philosophers and thinkers indulged in intellectual activity in both countries, questioning doctrines and ethical values. Ayurvedic concepts occur in Plato's writings, and the importance of breathing as practiced in India's Ayurvedic system was emphasized by Hippocrates.[6]

Lured by ambition and the lore of India's wealth, ivory, and peacocks, Alexander crossed the Hindu Kush Mountains in 326 BCE to enter India. Taking advantage of warring kings, he was well received by Ambhi, king of Taxila. However, Porus, a powerful ruler in the northwestern region, refused to surrender and fought Alexander near the Hydaspes River (now named Jhelum), where Porus was finally defeated. A proud king, Porus is recorded to have won the respect of Alexander. Defeated and gravely injured in the battle, he was asked by Alexander how he wished to be treated. He responded, "Like a king."

Alexander advanced across Punjab victoriously. However, much to his dismay, his exhausted and recalcitrant soldiers

---

6. Ayurveda is a Sanskrit word derived from *ayus* (life) and *vid* (knowledge). The fourth Veda (Atharva Veda) contained the ancient wisdom about sickness and healing upon which Ayurvedic treatment is founded. It contains dissertations on chants, herbs, and potions and provides spiritual and philosophical advice on how to live a healthy and purposeful life. The basic belief is that we are composed of five elements called Panchamahabhutas and Tridoshas. By correcting the balance within ourselves and in relation to the world around us, we can promote health. Supposedly, the Hindu Gods handed down the principles of Ayurveda to the seers.

stopped and refused to go any further. Weary of numerous battles and homesick, they rebelled. A mutiny ensued, and with heavy heart, after much oratory and pleading, Alexander turned homeward. He left behind a number of Greek soldiers who married local women and governed Alexander's conquests. Alexander's campaign from Greece and into India established and accelerated several trade routes between India and western Asia.

Destiny had denied him his dream of subduing the Magadhan Empire. As a visionary, Alexander dreamed of world unification, but his ambition was thwarted. After a spectacular saga of daring exploits, he died at the age of thirty-two in Babylonia on his return from India, even before he could reach Macedonia.

— 3 —
The First Indian Empire:
The Mauryan Dynasty
(322 BCE–320 CE)

Following Alexander's death, confusion ensued among the various governors of his empire in India. These lands swiftly fell into warring kingdoms under the hands of the local powers.

CHANDRAGUPTA MAURYA

Chandragupta Maurya (ruled 324–301 BCE), a man of very humble beginnings, took advantage of the conflicts to overthrow the king of Magadha and establish the first Indian Empire. Even his name is ambiguous, with some legends tracing the name Maurya to a lowly caste of peacock tamers, while others derive it from a warrior clan called the Moriyas. According to one legend, Chandragupta was born to the widow of a tribal chief who was killed in battle. As a child, he was kidnapped by a cowherd and sold to a hunter, who in turn sold him to Kautilya (also known as Chanakya), a Brahmin. Kautilya, a brilliant political adviser, came across Chandragupta playing on the street with a group of other children. The boy was pretending to be a king. Instantly, Kautilya was struck by the child's persona and quickly bought the boy from the hunter. Kautilya trained this young boy to become a skillful military leader, who then overthrew the remaining Greek rulers in Punjab before wresting power in Magadha.

Chandragupta Maurya was aided in his conquest by the shrewd wisdom of Kautilya, a Machiavellian adviser who was unscrupulous and treacherous but devoted to his king. It is said that Kautilya authored the *Arthashastra,* a treatise on the art of politics and government, as well as on the education and training of a king. Its teachings advised rulers to be on guard for spies who might disguise themselves as queens, ministers, merchants, barbers, soothsayers, mendicants, female house-holders, or wise men.

In an example of Kautilya's strategy, the young Chandragupta was able to overthrow the powerful Nandas after two failed attempts attacking the center of Magadha, the stronghold of the Nanda dynasty. After these defeats, Kautilya relates to Chandragupta the story of a little boy who, when given a dish of tasty and delicious food, immediately sticks his hand into the middle of the dish and burns his fingers. The moral drawn from this story suggests that the food will be hottest in the middle. It would be easier to eat from the sides first before encountering the middle, which would have cooled by then. And so, in his third attempt on Magadha, Chandragupta attacked and invaded the townships on the frontiers before conquering the center.

In a battle with Seleukos Nikator, a Greek viceroy who sought to recover Alexander's Indus conquests, Chandragupta Maurya emerged victorious (ca. 320 BCE). He acquired provinces in Afghanistan, and some say he even gained the daughter of Nikator. It is during this time that Nikator offered to Chandragupta's court the services of the Greek ambassador, Megasthenes. The writings of Megasthenes describe Chandragupta as a ruler who indulged his taste for finery and spectacle. He wore the finest of robes embroidered in gold, and he participated in elaborate processions involving elephants emblazoned with gold and silver. In these parades, marching female guards carried trees on which live birds perched. The king was also fond of watching fights between bulls, rams, rhinoceroses, and elephants. His sumptuous palace stretched nine miles in length and two miles in width. Its pillars were plated with gold, and skilled craftsmanship excelled in the royal residences.

Chandragupta Maurya's days were divided into sixteen periods ("hours") of ninety minutes each. In the first, he arose and prepared himself by meditation; in the second, he studied the reports of his agents and issued secret instructions; and in the third, he met with his councilors. In the fourth hour, he attended to state finances and national defense; in the fifth, he heard the petitions and suits of his subjects; and in the sixth, he bathed, dined, and read religious literature. He received taxes and tribute and made official appointments in the seventh hour. In the eighth hour, he met his council again and heard the reports of his spies and courtesans. The ninth hour was devoted to relaxation and prayer, while the tenth and eleventh hours were given to military matters and the twelfth to secret reports. In the thirteenth hour, the king indulged in an evening bath and a meal, and for the next three hours he slept—but never in the same bed twice! A suspicious despot, Chandragupta Maurya was always tormented by the shadow of danger. He surrounded himself with spies and informers, and all food was tasted in his presence.

Chandragupta Maurya ruled for twenty-four years. Wearying of suppressing constant revolts, and suffering from tensions and the burdens of a ruler and fear of assassination, he abdicated to become a Jain monk until he fasted to death. All of the warring kingdoms and tribesmen in North India were united under Maruyan rule, and the empire was extended to the south as far as Mysore by Chandragupta's son, Bindusara (296–273 BCE). Not much is known of Bindusura. His greatest contribution to India was his son Ashoka.

ASHOKA: ENLIGHTENED RULE

Chandragupta's grandson Ashoka's unsurpassed leadership brought the Mauryan Empire to its zenith. Ashoka (ruled 269–232 BCE), a remarkable and merciless warrior, subdued the kingdom of Kalinga, the last of the independent states. The aftermath of this slaughter, with a tally of one hundred thousand dead, found Ashoka stricken with revulsion and remorse. He underwent a profound conversion, ordered the prisoners freed, restored their lands, gave up hunting and the eating of meat, and sought peace. It may have been at this time that vegetarianism became popular in India. Abandoning war and conquest, Ashoka turned to Buddhism and devoted his life to its tenets of nonviolence (ahimsa), dharma, righteousness, and moral law. "Some historians have seen political and economic compulsions, rather than a genuine change of heart behind this sudden conversion. Ashoka's huge army was a drain on the economy, and the empire had grown too large for effective administration." (Shobita Punja, *The International Indian*.) Ashoka relaxed harsh laws and sponsored the building of rest houses, hospitals, and veterinary centers. Wells were dug, and thousands of trees and medicinal herbs were planted. A special class of high officers known as dharma ministers were appointed to look into the special needs of women and to help relieve their suffering. Ashoka held the first Great Council of the Buddhist clergy at Patliputra and propagated Buddhism by sending missionaries (sometimes his own son and daughter) to Sri Lanka, Burma, and Southeast Asia. It is as a result of Ashoka's patronage that Buddhism spread beyond the frontiers of India.

Ashoka ordered the construction of eighteen rocks and thirty polished sandstone pillars in the Persian style, engraved with five-thousand-word edicts on religion, government, and human behavior in Brahmi script (an antecedent of the Devanagari script of Sanskrit and modern Hindi). Masterpieces of engineering and craftsmanship, these monuments clearly state the philosophy of Ashoka: toleration, respect, duty to parents, abstinence from slaughter, compassion, and self-examination. The pinnacles of the pillars are decorated with animal sculptures. The most famous of these is the sculpture of the four lions of Sarnath, three of which have become the national symbol of modern India. The removal of one of these pillars by a Muslim ruler of Delhi in later years required the work of eighty-four hundred men pulling a cart with forty-two wheels. Of the eighteen rocks and thirty pillars, only ten pillars remain in good condition today. Ashoka also built eighty-four thousand dome-shaped Buddhist temples, or *stupas,* all over northern India. The stupas have been altered over time, but the most famous is the Great Stupa of Sanchi near Bhopal.

Ashoka also sent Buddhist missionaries to preach the concept of dharma in Egypt and Macedonia, and he maintained friendly relations with the rulers of the Hellenistic world. Indians learned much from Greek scientific inquiry in such fields as astronomy, astrology, and metallurgy. The Indians adopted the Greek calendar and skillfully executed Greek-style coins bearing the name and portrait of the ruling king. The reverse faces of

Sanchi Buddhist site, late first century BCE *(courtesy of Robert Arnett, India Unveiled).*

these coins bore representations of Greek Gods and mythological figures. The classical influence on coiffure and jewelry in India is fascinating. Like their Greek counterparts, women in Ajanta paintings are shown covering their hair with flowered scarves or bags made of cloth. An ear ornament consisting of a ring with two ball pendants fashionable in the Roman Empire is depicted in a painting in Ajanta in India. Ashoka's empire, it is said, even included Kashmir in the north, and there are suggestions of contact with South Indian kingdoms.

We know nothing of Ashoka's last years, when he was deposed by his own grandson and all powers were taken from him. Many awaited his death, including thousands of hunters and fishermen who rebelled against his edicts on preserving animal life. He died in 232 BCE.

END OF THE EMPIRE: FOREIGN INVADERS (185 BCE–320 CE)

The Mauryan Empire disintegrated after the death of Ashoka, and once again the various kingdoms broke away into fragments as a result of constant feuds, rivalries, and weak successors. Northern India was thus vulnerable to foreign invasions by the Greeks from Baktria; the Parthians from southeast of the Caspian Sea; and the Shakas or Scythians, the Kushans, and the Huans or Huns from Central Asia. These invaders from Central Asia were nomads and pastoral tribes who had fled their homeland for unknown reasons.

The Kushan Empire is remembered for King Kanishka (close to the first century CE), who, like Ashoka, converted to Buddhism, built monasteries, and supported sculptors and musicians from all over Asia. Kanishka established a kingdom extending from Kashmir and the Gandhara region to Benares in the east and Sanchi in the south. During his time, Buddhism spread to China. The Kushans imported and employed Greek artisans to decorate the monasteries with sculptures illustrating scenes from the life of Buddha, as described in the Jataka tales—stories of wisdom and morals, sacrifice, honesty and life of Buddha. These tales have a long tradition of being passed from generation to generation. The five hundred and forty seven tales were written in 483 BCE and form part of the literary treasures of Buddhism. They have been transmitted orally for centuries. *The Greedy Crow, The Quarrelsome Quails* and *The Jackal who saved the Lion* are still narrated today. The sculptures, influenced by Greek and Buddhist culture, are known as Gandhara art (Gandhara is the northwest frontier of India, where the carvings are found).

But unlike Ashoka, Kanishka remained an aggressor. He continued his conquests and campaigns until he came to a violent end, suffocated by his men in his own tent.

— 4 —
The Gupta Dynasty: The Golden Age of Indian Classicism
(320–647 CE)

A new Gupta dynasty arose at the beginning of the fourth century CE and established itself in the northern part of India. By marrying the daughter of the king of the powerful Licchhavi clan of Vaisali, Chandragupta I secured control of the Gangetic plains, which were essential for commerce, and established the Gupta Empire, proclaiming himself "King of Kings."

His son Samudragupta waged numerous victorious campaigns throughout India, expanding the Gupta Empire to Punjab in the north, to Assam in the east, and to the Deccan in the south. As a warrior, poet, and musician, Samudragupta is often compared to Alexander the Great. His son Ramagupta is remembered for a brief and weak reign. His brother, Chandragupta II (also known as Vikramaditya) assassinated Ramagupta, and led the Gupta Empire into its golden age of power and glory.

FLOURISHING OF LITERATURE AND THE ARTS

During Vikramaditya's reign, the Gupta Empire reached its zenith, annexing the whole of western India as far as the Arabian Sea, and thereby commanding the prosperous trade routes to the Western world. Accounts of his rule are indicated in the writings of the Chinese Buddhist pilgrims Fa-hien and Hiuen Tsang.

Religious liberty, wealth, and happiness abounded, and all over the country there were universities, monasteries, and hospitals. During Vikramaditya's reign, India's arts and sciences flourished. His was a peaceful and well-governed empire, where Buddhism was a strong force, although orthodox Brahminical Hinduism was gaining royal patronage.

The spectacular achievement in literary craftsmanship during this period is exemplified by one of the classics of world literature, *Shakuntala,* by the great poet and playwright Kalidasa, who was one of the "nine gems" of Vikramaditya's court. *Shakuntala* is a saga of love, marriage, separation, and reunion. The heroine, Shakuntala, is a forest nymph living in a hermitage. She bewitches the heart of King Dushyanta while he is hunting. The two of them enter what is known as a Gandharva marriage alliance, based on mutual consent. He eventually leaves her to attend to urgent affairs in the court, promising to return soon to reclaim her. He gives her his ring with the royal emblem. Shakuntala spends her days in the forest awaiting the king's return and dreaming about him, until a passing sage infamous for his short temper arrives at her doorstep. Lost in her thoughts of the king, Shakuntala does not attend to the sage. Enraged by this breach of hospitality, he curses her so that the person whom she was thinking about would forget her. Later, the sage relents and amends the curse by saying that King Dushyanta would remember her if he were shown the ring. Soon afterward, Shankutala finds herself with child and travels to the royal palace. On the way, she encounters a lake and is tempted to bathe in it. The ring slips from her finger and is swallowed by a fish. When she reaches the palace, the king does not remember her, and without the ring Shakuntala is unable to prove her identity. She returns to the forest and gives birth to a son. Years pass, and one day a fisherman arrives at the palace with the ring and the royal engraving. The king remembers Shakuntala and goes to the forest to claim his beloved.

Meghadutta (Cloud Messenger) is another celebrated Sanskrit poem by Kalidasa. With exquisite imagery, this saga of separation and longing describes the tormented plea of a *yaksha* (demon) to a cloud, imploring it to act as messenger and convey his message of yearning to his wife, who is separated from him by a curse.

Poetry, romantic comedies, and drama flourished during Vikramaditya's reign, and the *Mahabharata* was compiled and rewritten in the form we read today. Another record of a more developed form of Hinduism is found in the Puranas (Ancient Legends). These elaborate the worship of Vishnu (the Preserver) and Shiva, who represents the the cyclic process of destruction and regeneration.

The *Kamasutra* by Sage Vatsyayana is a fascinating narrative on the art of love and living. It elucidates the details of union, finding a partner, marriage, adultery, and use of intoxicants. Its rich invention regarding the varying dimensions of physical love has been acclaimed throughout the ages. Its investigation of this subject is so comprehensive that it includes the description of the qualities, characteristics, and temperaments of the various types of women of various lands; the days of greatest enjoyment for these women; the hours which give the highest enjoyment; various seats of passion for different kinds of men and women; astrology; marriage; and more.

Fables and fairy tales were very popular during the Gupta period. *Panchatantra* (*pancha* means five; *tantra* means books), a collection of stories in which animals act and speak like human beings, traveled from India to other corners of the world. Its themes and plots influenced "A Thousand and One Nights" and "Aesop's Fables," as well as later writers such as Chaucer and Boccaccio.

Courtly poets skillfully played with rhythms and lyrics using varying artifices. One poet composed verses without any sibilants, perhaps for a prince with a speech defect. Another wrote a poem that meant one thing when read left to right and another when read right to left. Poets challenged one another with riddles, long speeches, and puns, jousting verbally with their intelligence and virtuosity.

During this period, universities also flourished. The Buddhist monastery of Nalanda, near Patna in Bihar, became the most honored university in Asia, sometimes hosting as many as ten thousand monks and students on its premises. Gupta sculpture nourished a new school in Indian architecture. Magnificent sculptures in the cave temples of Ajanta and Ellora in Maharashtra give us an introduction to the skilled craftsmanship and imagination of the Gupta period's stonecarvers. The arts were inspired by religion, reinforcing the strong faith of generations of artists, patrons, and worshippers. The caves were forgotten for twelve hundred years and were rediscovered when British officers accidentally stumbled upon them during a tiger hunt (1819). The caves flaunt magnificent halls, temples, and pillars and are adorned with carved figures of elegant men, peacocks, jugglers, royal women, magicians, processions, acrobats, love scenes, feasting, elephants, and dancers.

Such temples incorporated the entire universe in stone. The inlaid sculpture on a pillared palace led a Chinese visitor

Gupta Dynasty, Ajanta caves (courtesy of Robert Arnett, India Unveiled*).*

to believe that the palace had been built by spirits in a way that no human hands of the world could accomplish. Buddhist lotus flowers vie with Hindu Gods, as well as demons, serpents, and dwarves from folk myths, all crowded together on a single sculpted panel. At the same time, illicit pleasure and temptation were also depicted as having tragic consequences. One fresco powerfully illustrates the story of shipwrecked travelers who come to an untimely end, lured by enticing ogresses disguised as seductive damsels. Because worshippers were often illiterate, one reason for such temples may have been to make clear the intricacies of their faith and its rituals. Such harmonious and vibrant ornamental detail characterizes this blessed period of time in India's history.

Mathematics was more advanced in India than in any other part of the world. Around 500 CE, the brilliant astronomer Aryabhatta calculated pi as 3.1416 and the length of the solar year as 365.358 days. He also determined that the Earth was a sphere rotating on its own axis and revolving around the Sun. In these discoveries, Aryabhatta predated Copernicus and Galileo by almost one thousand years. Through his theories, European scholars and mathematicians learned methods for calculating the areas of triangles, volumes of spheres, and square and cube roots.

When Vikramaditya died, his son Kumaragupta ruled for forty years in relative peace, passing the kingdom to his son Skandagupta, who spent his twelve-year rule under threat from the Huns of Central Asia. In 454 the Huns had settled in northern and western India. Weakened by this constant menace, the Gupta Empire crumbled, and North India, which was already a loosely built confederacy, fragmented into a number of separate Hindu kingdoms. But the Huns retreated by the end of the sixth century, when the Persians and Turks attacked them in Bactria.

HARSHAVARDHANA

The next bright light in Indian history was heralded by the ascension of Harshavardhana (ruled 606–647), who at age sixteen ascended to the throne of Thaneswar and sought to reunify all of North India. His empire ultimately stretched from Gujarat in the west to Bengal in the east and as far as Kashmir in the north. The Chinese Buddhist pilgrim Hsuan Tsang also notes accounts of the gifted scholar Harshavardhana in his narratives. Harshavardhana controlled his empire by traveling throughout the land and listening to the complaints of his people. A champion of all religions, he wrote religious plays and, surprisingly, two comedies about life in a harem. During Harshavardhana's reign, the Nalanda University of Buddhism continued to flourish, but Hinduism gained immense popularity.

It is during this era that the study of yoga was founded by Pantanjali. According to this school of Hindu philosophy, spirituality can be pursued by breath and posture exercises, as well as control of conduct and meditation.

The significant historical biography titled *Harshacharita,* or Life of Harsha, by court poet Bana, in Sanskrit, is an exemplary work that delineates Harsha as a remarkable ruler of indomitable energy and moderation. Harsha died without leaving an heir, and his kingdom rapidly disintegrated into small states.

5

The South Indian Kingdoms:
Dynasties and Temple Culture
(ca. 100 BCE–1565 CE)

THE ANDHRAS AND THE PANDYAS

A new dynasty, the Andhras (also known as the Satavahanas) was carving out an independent state in South India. There is a controversy whether the dynasty became independent at the end of the third century BCE or the first century BCE. The Satavahanas did however settle down in the second century CE, as evidenced by Saka coins in northwestern Deccan. The Telugu-speaking Andhras were a powerful race that controlled many towns and villages.

The Andhra kingdom stretched from coast to coast and dominated the Deccan plateau and much of central and western India. Between the Krishna and the Godavari Rivers, the Andhras built temples embellished with carvings and decoration. Ashoka's stupa at Sanchi was completely rebuilt by the end of the first century, making it perhaps one of the most impressive Buddhist temples in South East Asia. Most of them were razed during the nineteenth century, but some relics can be found in museums. The third century saw the decline of the Andhras.

Further south was Tamil Nadu, the land of the Dravidians, or Tamils. (Tamil was the predominant language of the Dravidian group.) It was shared between three warring kingdoms:

the Pandyas in Madurai, the Cheras on the southwestern coast, and the Cholas in Thanjavur at the turn of the last century BCE.

Pandya may have been derived from Pandu, the name of the royal family in the epic *Mahabharata.* Inscriptions reveal contact between the Pandyans and the Roman Empire, with a Pandyan king sending an ambassador to the court of Augustus Caesar in Rome. The Pandyans controlled the regions for many centuries. The Italian traveler Marco Polo is believed to have visited the Pandyan kingdom in 1288, returning to write elaborately of his travel in South India. Madurai, the Pandyan capital, is still one of South India's greatest and most revered temple cities.

Madurai was the center of Tamil literary culture and several *sangams* (assemblies of Tamil poets) were held there. Tamil was the first South Indian language to develop a literature of its own and it is thought by some to be older than Sanskrit. Anthologies of Tamil poetry were collected from hundreds of poets who attended the sangams. Two thousand poems have survived and are compiled in eight anthologies. The *Tolkappiyam,* the earliest Tamil grammatical treatise, is thought to have been written during this time.

Two epics tell of two courtesan dancers, Madhavi (*Silappadikaram,* or *The Jeweled Anklet*) and her daughter, Manimegelai, whose name is the title of the second poem. *Silappadikaram* was written by Ilango Adigal, the son of a Chera king. Kovalan, a young, handsome, rich merchant falls deeply in love with a royal courtesan, Madhavi. Although his wife Kannagi is devoted to him, he pursues the beauteous courtesan and has a daughter by Madhavi. He spends all his wealth

West gopuram, Meenakshi temple, Madurai (courtesy of Robert Arnett, India Unveiled*).*

on his new infatuation, becomes penniless, and returns to his wife. Their only wealth is a pair of anklets. Husband and wife then travel to the great city of Madurai to begin a new life. Kovalan goes to the marketplace to sell one of the anklets to obtain money. At that time, the queen and the king of the Pandyas had just been robbed of a similar anklet. The royal jeweler happens to see Kovalan with Kannagi's anklet and immediately seizes it and informs the king. Guards arrest Kovalan, who is then killed on the king's orders. Kannagi, consumed by rage, rushes to the king, carrying the remaining anklet in her hand as proof of her husband's innocence. The king realizes his folly and falls dead in intense remorse over the injustice. Kannagi is not appeased; she tears out her left breast in rage and with a potent curse sets the city of Madurai aflame. Weakened by the loss of blood, Kannagi dies and is reunited with Kovalan in heaven. Kannagi becomes revered as the patron Goddess of wifely loyalty and chastity.

The sequel, *Manimegelai,* is about the love of prince Udayakumaran for Madhavi and Kovalan's daughter, Manimegelai. In *Manimegelai,* the daughter of the courtesan makes an independent choice for life as a Buddhist nun and argues with great philosophical and religious conviction.

The Tamil kingdoms were legendary for their gold and precious jewels. Court life glittered with actors, musicians, and dancers. Devadasis (female temple dancers), literally "servants of the Gods," were an integral part of the South Indian culture. The devadasi was considered the wife of the God and a bearer of good fortune. Her presence at weddings, births, and naming ceremonies was considered extremely auspicious.

THE PALLAVAS AND THE CHOLAS

The conflicts of the three Tamil kingdoms left them weak and vulnerable to a new dynasty, the Pallavas, who appeared in Kanchipuram and entrenched themselves by 325 CE. There was lucrative trade between the Roman empire and South India in return for onyx and spices. Recent archaeological findings have discovered Roman coins of gold and copper in Madurai, Kerala, and Karnataka.

The temples in Kanchipuram, Mahabalipuram, and Tiruchirappalli (built by the Pallavas) and Madurai, the temple city of the Pandyas, are outstanding testaments to the architectural genius and religious fervor of the period between the fourth and eighth centuries. The temple became the social, religious, and educational center of a society that was becoming increasingly stratified by caste. In accordance with Vedic tradition, Brahmin priests conducted religious rites, while non-Brahmins were kept away from rituals. Kingship was believed to be of divine origin. Kings conformed to Brahmin traditions and bestowed high honor on the priests, believing them to be the link to the Omnipotent Brahma.

At this time, Adi Shankaracharya, (born in 805 CE) an intelligent Brahmin from Kerala, found the Vedic traditions and rituals to be abstruse and complex. He founded the Vedanta school of thought, which encouraged speculative thinking, debate, and discussion. He advocated that the world was illusion, *maya,* and that we humans cannot perceive reality unless we control our senses. Only asceticism can help man to achieve knowledge of the divine. He traveled all over India, attracted a devoted following, wrote treatises, debated with philosophers

Descent of the Ganges, Mahabalipuram, Pallava Dynasty (courtesy of Robert Arnett, India Unveiled*).*

and at the age of thirty-two retired to a cave in the Himalayas near Kedarnath. His philosophy still garners respect and popularity today.

During this time, worship of the Vedic Gods gradually declined and was replaced by veneration of the Hindu Trinity: Brahma (creator), Vishnu (preserver), and Shiva (destroyer in the form of the Lingam or the phallus, denoting male creative energy). It is also believed that St. Thomas traveled to India in the first century, spreading Christianity among the people of the Malabar Coast.

There is much debate about the arrival of the first Jews, (some scholars say 10,000) in India who may have come in 72 AD after the destruction of the Second Temple in Jerusalem or they may have arrived in the sixth century BCE when they were persecuted and exiled by Nebuchhanazar. But the royal gift of rights and privileges inscribed on copper plates were given to them by the local ruler, Bhaskara Ravi Varman, in 1000 CE and they remained in Kerala, settling in Cochin. There was a mass emigration back to Israel between 1948–1955. Today there are only 50 Cochin Jews remaining in Kerala.

The Cholas overthrew their Pallava masters in the ninth century. Under Raja Raja Chola I (ruled 985–1014 CE), they invaded northern Sri Lanka, destroyed the capital (Anuradhapura), and established themselves there for a short period. At its zenith, the Chola empire extended across the peninsula to the south of modern Goa and Orissa. The Cholas were great patrons of art, literature, and architecture. They excelled in the art of bronze sculpture and erected tributes to the Gods in the form of elaborately decorated temples.

The origins of many of these temples are associated with fascinating legends. One legend regards the largest temple in India, the temple of Srirangam in Tiruchirappalli. This is one of the hundred and eight pilgrimage shrines of Lord Vishnu. Surrounded by seven concentric walls and twenty-one *gopurams* (towers), Srirangam enshrines the image of Vishnu reclining on a massive serpent. The walls of this magnificent temple are adorned by one thousand sculptured pillars. According to legend, the sage Vibhisana was carrying the idol of Vishnu across the country to Sri Lanka when he rested it on the ground for a few moments. When he tried to lift the image again, it appeared to be fixed to the Earth and would not be moved. A temple was then built around this idol. Even Ramanuja lived here for many years and was buried at the site.

The Akhilandeswari Temple in Tiruchi has another intriguing story of its origins. In the forest where the Shiva Lingam was situated, an elephant used to offer prayers each day, pouring fresh water brought in its trunk from the nearby Cauvery River. Another devotee, a spider, upon finding decaying leaves and flowers falling from the trees above onto the Lingam, built a strong web over it so that the leaves were caught in the web. The elephant was annoyed on seeing the web and trampled on it. The enraged spider bit the elephant by entering its trunk. The elephant died, and the spider also perished because it was unable to get out of the trunk. Upon finding that both devotees had come to a tragic end, Lord Shiva blessed the spider, which was then reborn as the Chola king, Kochenganan. He is credited with building seventy Shiva temples and five Vishnu temples. The elephant was also blessed and continues to be used in service for processions and rituals in South Indian temples.

Raja Raja Chola I (985–1014) brought stability to the Chola kingdom. He is also remembered for having restored from obscurity the brilliant *Tevaram* hymns of the Shaivite Nayanars (followers of Shiva). These Shaivite saints steeped themselves in hymns, prayers, and devotions emphasizing the connection between man and God, rather than ritual practice. This was to be the basis of Ramanuja's Bhakti movement.

It is believed that one day Raja Raja Chola heard these mystic hymns of the Shaivite saints and was enchanted. When he heard of several others like them, he ordered an intensive search. The hymns and lyrics were eventually found in the manuscript room of a temple. The priests declared that the hymns could not be given to the king but only to the authors, who were of course dead. In a brilliant move, Raja Raja Chola ordered the creation of statues of the three authors—Appar, Sambandar, and Sundarar—who had first sung these hymns in Pallava times. The king had the statues placed in the manuscript room of the temple. The priests handed over the dilapidated hymns, and today the religious lyrics are still sung with devotion.

Raja Raja Chola was a pious man and expressed his faith in the Gods by building magnificent temple complexes at Thanjavur, the capital of the Chola kingdom. The building techniques of his engineers and artisans were unmatched for centuries. He created a temple, the Brihadeeshwara, of such proportions as no one had ever witnessed. Woodworkers, painters, and sculptors brought to life Gods, Goddesses, animals, demigods, and demons on and within the walls. Icons are cast in silver, gold, copper, bronze, brass, and panchaloha (an amalgam of gold, silver, zinc, tin, and copper). Facing the main shrine is a twenty-five-ton, monolithic Nandi bull (the steed of Shiva). In the center of the courtyard, a tower (*vimanam*) rises to the sky. Layers of decorated stone moldings support the floor of this sanctum. The architects distributed the weight of the tower between a pair of parallel walls two stories high, and they converted the corridors in between into an art gallery on two levels with painted murals of forest scenes and images of Shiva. On the second level, where the dance hall is located, one hundred and eight South Indian classical dance poses are engraved with descriptions. The grand and opulent tower appears to be suspended in space; it was created with such ingenuity that its crown does not cast a shadow on the ground.

The remains of the temples are a cultural and artistic record of those times, with their massive gateways, central courtyards encircled by heavy stone walls, rectangular pyramids, and outer structures of brick covered with stucco carvings. The temples soon became cities and encompassed whole towns. Markets and merchants proliferated within the temples, and special halls were built for religious festivals. Pilgrims came from throughout the land, and all of the people performed ritual immersions for themselves and the Gods in huge stone pools. In this manner, daily life and religion bonded and merged easily and naturally.

The eleventh-century Tamil Brahmin philosopher Ramanuja born in 1017 was another revered reformer of Vedic tradition. He disagreed with Shankara's theory that knowledge was the primary means of salvation. Surrendering to God was much more effective and reliable. The devotional movement that he founded was known as Bhakti. Ramanuja's God was a God of love and forgiveness. He pleaded for the acceptance of Shudras in the temples, but without much success. However, the orthodox Brahmins became aware of these issues and recognized the need to compromise.

THE CHERAS

Political developments on the Kerala coast were far more restrained, with the Chera kings having little political ambition. Since the land was rich in produce, the Cheras did not need to conquer new territories. The earliest reference to the Chera Dynasty of the Malabar Coast is made in the Sangam literature of the second century BCE. Later, in the ninth century CE, the Kulasekaras, descendants of the Cheras, came to power and remained rulers until the twelfth century. They were greatly influenced by priests and astrologers. From their five strategic ports, a flourishing trade in pepper and sandalwood continued with the west until the sixth century. Coins of Byzantine emperors have been discovered in Kerala. The port at Quilon was visited by Arabs, Chinese, and European travelers. During the rule of the Cheras, a unique Nair (administrative and warrior class) family structure was established based on the matrilineal system (*marumakkathyam*), according to which the wife and daughter, rather than the son, inherited property. Military prowess was encouraged by the system of Kalaris, or schools teaching agility, gymnastics, and the martial arts.

Another community, the Namboodiris (priestly class), followed a patriarchal system under which only the eldest son could marry. The younger sons could have relations, called *sambandham,* with Nair women. The *tharawad,* or ancestral home, was Nair dominated and always associated with a temple.

Meanwhile trade with Persia, Arabia, China, and Sri Lanka proved lucrative, with exports of perfumes, ebony, camphor, textiles, and jewels, as well as elephants and horses. En route to China, traders stopped at the ports of Burma and in various parts of Java, Indonesia, Malaysia, and even Cambodia. Buddhist missionaries arrived in China, and monasteries were established. Chinese Buddhists were coming to India to study. Caravans of oxen and camels traversed the country, carrying produce and products that included coins for barter.

THE HOYSALAS AND THE VIJAYANAGARS

Two new powers emerged in the thirteenth and fourteenth centuries: the Hoysalas of Belur and Halebid, west of Bangalore; and the Vijayanagars of northern Karnataka. The garden city of palaces, pavilions, baths, temples, bazaars, and elephant stables—Vijayanagar (City of Victory)—in Andhra Pradesh became the capital of a southern Hindu empire that lasted from 1336 to 1565. This empire was founded by two brothers, Harihara and Bukka, who had been taken captive by Mohammed Tughlaq, the Muslim ruler of North India. In captivity they converted to Islam. When there was a rebellion in the southern Hindu regions, they were sent to quell the disturbance. There they took control, converted back to Hinduism, and became independent.

Vijayanagar reached its height of prosperity in 1509–1529 with Krishna Deva Raya, a great military leader. Vijayanagar traded with Burma, China, Persia, Africa, Portugal, and Malaysia, attracting Italians, Persians, and other foreigners to the city. These dynasties lasted until the Muslims began their conquest of India, sweeping down from the north.

— 6 —

The Rajput Era: Clans,
Campaigns, and Chivalry
(647–1296 CE)

The period between the death of Harshavardhana and the Muslim conquest of India may be called the Rajput era (seventh–twelfth centuries CE), though they were to rise again in later centuries. During this period, North India came under the domination of the warrior Rajput clans, who probably were descendants of the Central Asian Shakas and Huns who invaded North India during the late Gupta period. The foreign origin of the Rajputs is often contested by Brahmanic scholars, who prefer to believe that the Rajputs were pure Aryans.

According to the *Angikula* legend, Parasurama, the sixth avatar of Vishnu, had destroyed all the Kshatriya warrior clans in an act of vengeance. However, the Brahmins needed the warrior caste to defend them. They offered prayers and burned an enormous fire (*Agnikula*, or fire pit) for forty days. Out of this fire pit emerged the four Rajput heroes who would each create a separate Rajput clan: the Chauhans, the Solankis or Chalukyas, the Parmaars, and the Pratiharas. They became known as Rajputs from *Raj-Putra*, Sanskrit for "Son of King"— that is, of royal blood. Still others maintain that the Rajputs were of foreign descent and that the legendary fire represents a rite of purgation to cleanse the foreigners and allow them to enter into Hinduism.

The clans established themselves as local kings in north-western and central India. Contact with the outside world decreased, trade with the West diminished, imperial titles were bestowed on the kings, and the Rajputs rose to political importance.

The Rajputs were renowned for their chivalry, bravery, passion, and devotion to war. They fought against one another incessantly, and they valiantly opposed Muslim rule. Songs and legends of the Rajputs' valor, heroism, and readiness to die for their beliefs still resound in India today.

The Rajput code resembled the medieval European ideal of chivalry as elaborated in Arthurian tales. Courtesy, honor, and courage were paramount, along with respect for women, mercy for the helpless, and adherence to ceremonial rituals. One particularly spellbinding legend is based on the Turkish conquest of the city of Chitor. In the story, the Mohammedan invader, Alauddin of the Khilji dynasty (1296) fell in love with the beauteous Rajput queen, Padmini, wife of Rana Ratan Singh of Mewar. Alauddin threatened to besiege Chitor if the queen was not surrendered to him. On being refused, Alauddin agreed to withdraw if he were allowed to see Padmini in a mirror. He was shown her face and fell even more deeply in love. Alauddin gathered his forces to invade Chitor. The Rajput men went to war and were defeated. When the news reached Padmini, she and all the women of the fort committed *jauhar*, a type of ritual suicide in which all the women go to their deaths on a funeral pyre while the men open the gates with the aim of dying in battle. When Alauddin entered the city victorious, every man was dead and every woman had burned herself to death. Only thus could the honor of the Rajputs be preserved. Jauhar was committed three times in the history of Chitor before the fort was abandoned.

A Rajput.

The Hindi, Marathi, and Gujarati languages flourished under Rajput rulers. Another writer, Chand Bardai, wrote the *Prithvirajraso* in the vernacular, extolling the heroic deeds of the Rajput, Prithiviraj Chauhan. He fell in love with the daughter of his bitter enemy, the king of Kanauj. When the king summoned her suitors to a gathering, Prithiviraj was not invited. Instead, to humiliate him, the king had placed a statue of him by the door. The princess walked up to the statue and placed her garland around it, symbolizing her choice of husband. Prithiviraj, who had been hiding nearby, rode in with his horse, like the Scottish Lochinvar, and carried her off in true heroic fashion.

Creativity and the arts blossomed in the realm of religion as well. During the twelfth century, the Bengali poet Jayadeva composed the mystic erotic *Gita Govinda* (Song of Krishna) in Sanskrit, immortalizing the love and dalliance of Radha and Lord Krishna. The cities of Mewar, Udaipur, and Chitor are examples of the level of architectural excellence reached in Rajput India. The Kandariya Mahadeo Temple of Shiva, the marble temples of the Jains in Rajasthan, the temples of Bhubaneshwar, and the shrine of Puri in Orissa are all testament to the artistic craftsmanship that flourished during this period. At the magnificent sun temple at Konarak, the entire temple is in the shape of a massive stone chariot, the vehicle of the sun God, Surya.

Ironically, this heroic age is also called the "Dark Age of India" because of the rigid caste system enforced by the Rajputs. While the caste system was not very prominent during the beginning of this era, it soon became a central element of social life. Child marriage also was rampant during this time, along with the practice of polygamy, the persecution of Buddhists, the glorification of sati, and jauhar. It is believed that for the kings to survive they had to appease the Brahmins who often had helped them come to power, and thus the Brahmins earned legal and religious sway over kingdom after kingdom. They were venerated, exempted from taxation, and given grants of land and wealth. In many ways this period parallels the Middle Ages of western Europe, with its social stratification and lack of centralized authority.

One of the celebrated figures in Rajput history is Mira Bai, who was married at the age of thirteen in accordance with tradition. A devout worshipper of Lord Krishna, she is believed to have said that it was impossible to engage in marital responsibilities with her husband when she was already married to God. Following the early death of her husband, Mira Bai abandoned all custom by refusing to comply with committing the widow's customary sati (self-immolation) rite, much to the horror of her in-laws. Instead, she left their home and wandered throughout Rajasthan, preaching and singing her self-composed devotional songs to Lord Krishna. Today some one hundred *Mira bhajans* (devotional songs) in praise of Krishna are still sung throughout India.

— 7 —
Turkish Invasion and Rule: The Rise of Islam
(647–1526 CE)

From 610 CE onward, a new religion was making its appearance in Arabia: Islam, or "submission to the will of God" in Arabic. Its followers were called Muslims. Muhammad, a merchant of Mecca, founded the religion and was regarded by its adherents as a prophet who received revelations from God (called "Allah") in the form of visions. These visions were codified in the Koran, the holy book of the Muslims. The Islamic statement of faith remains, "There is no God but Allah, and Muhammad is his prophet." The monotheistic religion also calls on all Muslims to give alms to the poor, to pray five times a day while facing Mecca, to fast in daylight during the ninth lunar month, and to make a pilgrimage to Mecca. Islamic codes taught that God was absolute and could not be represented in any form or image. They condemned caste restrictions and advocated a single universal religion.

Muhammad's successors were rulers who fought wars of conquest and spread their religion from Arabia to North Africa, Spain, and Persia, as well as across Asia toward India. Arab merchants' tales of India's wealth also lured would-be conquerors. The earliest invasions occurred in the eighth century when the Arabs penetrated Sindh, in modern Pakistan (712 CE). Internal conflict and war, as well as the pacifism preached by nonviolent religions like Buddhism and Jainism, had left the Indian Hindus unprepared for the onslaught. This isolated occurrence left the Arabs with territory in Sindh, but three hundred peaceful years would pass before Islamic invaders sought to disturb the rest of India. This time, the effect of the persistent, powerful invasions would dramatically and permanently alter the course of Indian history. In the tenth century, Turks from Central Asia established themselves in Afghanistan and from there initiated the first significant Muslim invasion of India in 997.

Mahmud of Ghazni, from the kingdom of Ghazni (modern Afghanistan), was known as the Sword of Islam and was said to have led seventeen bloody campaigns into India. He was twenty-six years of age when he first led raids to destroy and loot Thaneswar, Mathura, Kanauj, Nagarkot, and Kathiawar. The invaders razed magnificent temples; stole treasuries, spices, and precious stones; and raped and abducted women. Muslim chronicles tell us that in Kangra emeralds, diamonds, rubies, and pearls were plundered, and opulent cities were sacked. The expedition against the Somnath Temple in Gujarat is remembered for the dreadful carnage of its people, who were taken as slaves or crushed under the feet of elephants. With fourteen golden domes, the Somnath Temple was a magnificent work of science and architecture, with the Shiva Lingam appearing to be suspended in midair due to a magnetic field. The entire temple was destroyed by the invaders. By the end of Mahmud's reign, Punjab and northwestern India were under Muslim rule, leaving the rest of India still independent. Ghazni became one of the world's largest centers of Islamic culture by the eleventh century. Ironically, Mahmud of Ghazni is remembered for his patronage of Persian poets such as Ansari and Firdausi.

Shrewd, unrelenting **Sultan Muhammad of Ghur**, a Turk, arrived in Sind and Punjab in 1175 and made his first attack on India to plunder the land and establish a kingdom. He conquered Punjab, Peshawar, and Lahore and attacked the united Rajput kingdoms in the Gangetic Plain. Under the supreme command of the legendary Prithiviraj Chauhan, the Rajputs fought aggressively against the Turko-Afghan Muslims. Prithiviraj won the first battle in 1191, but he lost to the Muslims at Panipat in 1192. When Prithiviraj was executed, in true Rajput tradition, Prithiviraj's wife (whom he had loved and taken away from his enemy) fell on her husband's pyre and perished in the flames.

When Muhammad of Ghur was assassinated in Lahore in 1206, his slave, lieutenant Qutb-ud-Din, a Turk, became ruler of Delhi. He founded the **Mamluk (Slave) Dynasty**, putting Delhi under the rule of Turkish and Afghan sultans. For some 320 years, five Turko-Afghan dynasties ruled from Delhi: Mamluk (1211–1290), Khilji (1290–1320), Tughlaq (1320–1413), Sayyid (1414–1450), and Lodhi (1451–1526). During his reign, Qutb-ud-Din built the famous Qutb-ud-Din mosque and Qutb Minar in Delhi. The celebrated monument is fifty-two feet at its base and two-hundred-sixty feet high. Carved with verses from the Koran, these symbols of Islam's triumph over the Hindus were named in memory of the saint Qutb-ud-Din Ushi, who lies buried nearby.

The role of women in the Muslim world was enhanced by the legend of **Sultan Raziya** (ruled 1237–1240). As sovereign, she was a just, wise patron of the learned and a skilled warrior. She succeeded her father, Ilutmish, who ruled Delhi for twenty-five years, and her profligate brother, Ruknnidin, who was known for his excesses and debauchery and was deposed

Qutb Minar.

after just seven months' rule. Raziya abandoned female dress and rode at the head of the army. Even though she was in power for a mere three years, as the only Muslim woman ever to rule in India she became a much-romanticized figure. She was resented for being a woman and was murdered by her own palace guard. After the death of Raziya, Amir I-Shikar (Lord of the Hunt) let loose a reign of terror. He believed he had the divine right to rule and took on the title of Zil-i-Illahi, or the shadow of God on Earth.

Genghis Khan, a young Mongol chief born in 1162, gradually acquired supreme power over Mongolia, Northern China, Turkistan, Samarkhand, and Bukhara. He destroyed the inhabitants of Afghanistan and Ghazni, occupied Peshawar, and attempted to make a stand on the Indus river (1221). However, he was defeated, although some historians say he fell from a horse and died. India was spared the horrors that befell Central Asia at his hands.

In 1290, the Khilji, an Afghan tribe, seized the throne, thus ending the dynasty of the Turkish slave-sultans of Delhi. Another despot but an able leader of the **Khilji Dynasty** was Alauddin (1296–1316), who regarded himself as a second Alexander the Great. He was not only arrogant and cruel but also illiterate. For twenty years Alauddin crushed the Hindus, reducing them to poverty and bringing the Muslim faith to India's southernmost tip. He is said to have died at the hands of his slave eunuch general. Alauddin's first two sons were blinded by this general, Malik Kafur. His third son, Mubarak Khan, bribed Malik Kafur's agents and rose to the throne. Four years later, Mubarak Khan was killed by his own minister; in turn, the minister was killed within four months by **Ghiyas ud-din Tughlaq**, the son of a Muslim Turk court slave and a Hindu Jat (Sikh) woman.

Ghiyas's son, **Muhammad Tughlaq** (1325–1351) seized control of northern India and extended his dominion deep into southern India. He controlled twenty-four provinces but was never sure of their total allegiance. Muhammad was an accomplished visionary who saw India as a united country. But he was also an eccentric, indulging in mad schemes and barbarous acts that earned him the title of Pagla Tughlaq (the mad Tughlaq). He committed frightful massacres, organizing manhunts, and yet he was eloquent and proficient in Arabic, Persian, logic, mathematics, and Greek philosophy. He even abstained from drink and was distinguished for his gallantry. He was succeeded by his cousin, **Firuz Shah**, who ruled intelligently for thirty-seven years, reversing all taxation laws and building gardens and parks. Following him, a series of ineffective rulers seized the throne of Delhi while the nobility skirmished with one another. This lasted until the arrival in 1398 of **Timur the Lame (Tamerlane)**, a Mongol chieftain from Central Asia, who defeated India's rulers, sacked Delhi, and began a violent butchery of Hindus. Interested in neither conversion nor a kingdom, Timur returned to Samarkand with India's riches.

The fifteenth century saw two dynasties: the Turkish **Sayyids** (1414–1450) were displaced by an Afghan dynasty, the Lodhis. **Sikander Lodhi** (1489–1517), a scholar and poet, encouraged the arts and stimulated interest in the mingling of Hindu and Muslim literature and art. He was also known to have abhorred idolatry (including forms of worship practiced by Hindus), and he destroyed many temples. His son Ibrahim Lodhi, the last of the Lodhi monarchs, was a suspicious autocrat who antagonized his Afghan chiefs, inspiring rebellion. Paranoid, he began to doubt the loyalty of his own brother and killed him. To enforce his control over his nobles, Ibrahim is said to have shown one of them a particular room in which insubordinate chiefs were hung from the walls. Horrified, the nobles invited **Zahir-ud-din Muhammad Babur**, ruler of Kabul (Afghanistan) to invade India in 1526.

During this period of Turkish and Afghan rule, a new language, Persian, deposed Sanskrit from its position as the official language in north India. Indo-Muslim culture saw the flowering of a new literary genre with the cultivation of Persian literature. Chroniclers documented the rise of Muslim power, while the poet Amir Khusrau (1253–1325) is still highly acclaimed as the father of Indo-Muslim culture. Books were illustrated with fine, delicate, miniature paintings. The most visible change on the Indian landscape was a stunning new architecture. Mosques and mausoleums boasted domes, minarets, and sweeping arches. Religious buildings, forts, and palaces were adorned with geometric and floral patterns, as well as with texts from the Koran.

*The Moghul Emperor Jehangir (ruled 1605–1627 CE),
(courtesy of www.exoticindia.com).*

~ 8 ~

The Moghul Dynasty: Political Ambitions and the Impact of Islam
(1526–1858 CE)

The brilliant Moghul period was a fascinating and highly significant epoch in Indian history. This empire endured for three centuries, with seven generations of extraordinary rulers whose roots lay in Central Asia (the word *Moghul* comes from "Mongol"). The Moghul legacy includes the exquisite Taj Mahal, the grandeur of the Red Fort, the desolate city of Fatehpur Sikri, landscaped gardens, dress, food, and customs based on the teachings of the Koran. (For example, pork and alcohol were forbidden, and surplus food always was to be shared with the poor.)

The beautiful minarets commemorating the triumphs of the rulers over the Hindus are masterpieces of architecture. Several paintings illustrate emperors reading, writing, and discoursing with scholars. The cloistered life of the *zenana* (women's quarters) is also represented in paintings of ladies passing the time playing games and applying makeup. Other leisure activities took place in music rooms with painted ceilings filled with drums and other instruments, as well as ostentatious elaborate furniture. Hunting scenes depict falconer's gloves, hawks, horses and other animals, and plants. The paintings are a matchless record of everyday activities ranging from the intimate and personal to official duties. They depict warriors brandishing swords and mounted on horses, and there are magnificent portraits of rulers on splendid thrones smoking hookahs and inspecting horses. Consummately skilled carpet weavers created silk and wool pieces with over one thousand knots per square inch. The carpets depict rocks, water, and flowering plants.

The history of the Moghuls and their influence on India is also a record of hatred and intrigue under the shadow of the sword. It includes assassinations, court politics, religious intolerance, ravenous ambition, and anarchic rebellions.

Babur (the Tiger)

With the ferocious warrior blood of Timur from his father's side and Ghenghis Khan on his mother's side, Babur (ruled 1526–1530 CE) swept into India. In half a day he defeated Ibrahim Lodhi's army with a cavalry of twelve thousand soldiers and artillery in the historic battle of Panipat. Much to the horror of the Afghan nobles, instead of returning to his homeland, Babur decided to stay, thereby laying the foundation of the Moghul Dynasty. Thus ended Afghan dominion, with Babur occupying Delhi. Now the fortune of India lay in his hands.

Babur then triumphed over the brave and chivalrous Rajputs (who were led by one-eyed, one-armed Rana Sanga, the ruler of Mewar) and made himself master of the Gangetic plain by 1529. It is said that the rumors about the Rana's brave army made the Muslim soldiers uneasy. One of Babur's astrologers even predicted defeat for Babur. Enraged by the weakness of the people, Babur is said to have beheaded the astrologer and vowed never to drink wine again if he triumphed in battle.

Babur defeated the Rana with the use of brilliant war tactics and artillery, which was new to the Indians. The Rajputs were left divided and weak, and the sovereignty of India was now firmly in the hands of the Moghuls.

Babur was a man of great sensibility and taste. A brilliant scholar and formidable military ruler with a magnetic personality, he waged many battles with the Indian princes. Legend tells us that he rode one hundred and sixty miles on horseback in one day. He died at the young age of forty-eight, having spent his last years writing poems and his memoirs, a frank self-portrait. They depict his zest for life and love of Persian gardens, which he landscaped. Despite being a man of blood and iron, he had a tender appreciation of the beauties of nature. As he traveled through India, he complained of the lack of grapes, ice water, good food, and academies, and said that people were unfriendly. He longed for the Afghan hills of his birth.

When his only son Humayun fell ill, Babur asked God to take his life instead of his son's. The prayer was answered. Humayun recovered, and Babur died soon afterward. Another story suggests that Babur was poisoned by the mother of Ibrahim Lodhi. His body was buried in the gardens of his home in Kabul.

Humayun

Humayun (ruled 1530–1556 CE) lost the territories his father had won. Humayun (which means fortunate) was an educated ruler, skilled in mathematics and astronomy. But he lacked political wisdom and the resolute nature of his father. He was constantly outwitted by his enemies and vulnerable to treachery. His army—a conglomerate assembly of Turks, Indians, Afghans, and Persians—was not always loyal to him. He was also an opium addict. Ultimately, he lost all his provinces and therefore was unable to destroy the new threatening powers in the east. He soon found himself a fugitive from Sher Khan, the new Afghan leader, who defeated him in 1540.

Humayan wandered from kingdom to kingdom in exile, seeking aid from various chiefs of Sind and Mewar without success. In 1555, Humayun secured Persian help to cross the Indus River and reoccupy Delhi. A year later, it is said, he died in a fall from the stairs of his library, leaving his thirteen-year-old son, Akbar, to fight for his inheritance. His wife raised a magnificent tomb in honor of his memory, replete with gardens, fountains, and pools of water. The domed tomb is a precursor of the Taj Mahal.

AKBAR

The young Akbar (ruled 1556–1605 CE), guided by his guardian Bairam Khan, met the challenge of the Hindu general, Hemu, at the second battle of Panipat. In 1560, Akbar dismissed Bairam Khan. Akbar ruled his own government, conquering one territory after another: Gujarat (which was ruled by the Moghuls for one hundred and eighty-five years), the port of Surat with its trade with Arabia and Egypt, and Bengal with its abundance of silk and rice, followed by Kashmir, Orissa, Sind, and Jaipur. Akbar ruled the Moghul Empire for forty-nine years with absolute power. He slowly expanded the empire by diplomatically marrying Rajput princesses, permitting Hindus to practice their religion, and stabilizing the regions. Realizing that the country was becoming multireligious, he appointed Rajput chiefs as partners in the empire, investing them with titles. Religious toleration and freedom of worship helped in the integration of Hindus and Muslims. Akbar instituted land reforms by rewarding his lieutenants lavishly with lands whose revenues supported the troops. The guardian of all religions, he ended the destruction of Hindu temples, fostered arts and letters, encouraged Hindu and Muslim painters and poets, and attempted to unify Hindus and Muslims. He abolished the hated *jizya* poll tax Hindus paid for retaining their faith. The Hindus preferred this to being forcibly converted or condemned to death.

Inheriting the intelligence, zeal, and enthusiasm of his forefathers, Akbar not only inspired allegiance and loyal service, he was possibly one of the wisest and most cultured of all kings.

Hunting was an important sport for Akbar. He hunted in broad daylight, with so many comrades and retainers the party resembled an army on the move. The hunt (or *kamargha*) for tigers, leopards, and elephants might have served the function of military maneuvers, preparing men for battles to come. The biggest kamargha that ever was staged took place in Lahore when fifty thousand beaters worked for a month to drive the game into a circle ten miles around in circumference, for the convenience of the hunters. Women of the imperial household often accompanied the men on hunting expeditions for antelope, pigs, and deer. Akbar also loved *chaugan*, a kind of hockey with the player on horseback, as well as *ishqbazi*, competitive pigeon races.

Akbar fostered in his subjects a love of aesthetics. The art of miniature painting with delicate and embellished depictions of individuals, animals, birds, and flowers reached its zenith during this period. Often, two or three artists collaborated, leading to speculation over who was the real creator of the miniature. Characteristics of this art form included the element of surprise, delicacy of workmanship, a set framework, and a finely detailed and evocative quality. The average size worked out to ten inches by six inches, and within this constricted area, historical legends and elaborate visual depictions were painstakingly embellished. A painting was seen as the equivalent of a written page. It was read from left to right and from top to bottom. It often required intent viewing, as the following story illustrates.

A master painter once painted the "Expectant Heroine" (Utka Nayika). The young maiden stands in a clearing of the forest, full of longing and expectation, resting a bejeweled arm on a flowering tree, forefinger lightly touching her lips, with a puzzled look on her face. The painter shared this with his friends and asked them what the young woman was pondering. Everyone looked at the painting and offered lofty reasons and conjectures. Maybe she was wondering what had delayed her lover. Had she come to the wrong place for the tryst? The master painter finally revealed the reason for the woman's expression. He told his friends to look closely at the bracelet that she was wearing on her left arm. It had alternating rubies and pearls and one of the pearls was missing. The young woman was wondering where it had fallen. A closer look would reveal the gem close to her feet where the painter had painted it.

Elaborate dinners were an important element of leisure. These were grand meals with thirty dishes, followed by the Moghul custom of relaxing in the landscaped perfumed gardens while the wine flowed.

A great lover of music, Akbar was a patron of musicians and singers like Baiju Bawra, and Sur Das, as well as Mian Tan Sen, who is credited with stopping the flow of the Jamuna River with his song. We are also told that his singing could make the clouds shower rain. Tan Sen was one of the "nine gems" of Akbar's court. The other eight excelled as scholars, poets, translators, administrators, and generals. The wittiest of them all was Birbal. Legends and stories about Birbal's quick wit have entertained the Indian people for four hundred years. With humor and surprise endings, the Birbal Tales reveal timeless morals. Hindi literature also became popular, and perhaps one of the most important figures was Tulsi Das (1532–1623), one of the greatest poets. Hindu texts were studied and translated from Sanskrit into Persian, while the historian Abul Fazl and poet laureate Faizi were regarded as national treasures.

Ironically, Akbar never learned to read or write, but he established colleges at Agra, Lahore, Delhi, and Fatehpur Sikri. Fatehpur Sikri (City of Victory) was built by Akbar between 1570 and 1585. According to legend, Akbar did not have a male heir, so he made a pilgrimage to Sikri to visit Salim Chisti, a holy man. Chisti foretold the birth of Akbar's first son, Salim (In Gratitude). To commemorate the birth of Salim, Akbar transferred his capital from Agra to Sikri (later known as Fatehpur Sikri) twenty-four miles away. Here he built a splendid sandstone city, comprising a grand and delicate composition of public buildings, bath houses, palaces, and temples. Interspersed were terraces and gardens, as well as an island stage for court music set within a pool and surrounded by four bridges. The Hall of Private Audience (Diwan I Khas) is unique with an enormous central pillar, resembling a stone palm tree laden with exotic fruit, supporting a throne. In 1585 Akbar abandoned the city because the supply of water proved inadequate or polluted. The tomb of Salim Chisti remains, and even today women visit his shrine to pray for a child.

Religion intrigued Akbar. He summoned theologians of all faiths: Brahmins, Jains, Zoroastrians, Jesuits, and Muslims. Akbar also carried on stimulating discussions and debates with Islamic Sufi mystics. The Sufis had come to India with the establishment of Turkish power and believed that mystical union with God could be achieved through deep devotion and love of the Divine. They lived in seclusion and were often regarded as heretics due to their hypnotic rituals, such as dancing, leading them into a trancelike state. Their language became highly symbolic, and they formed an order under a *pir* (the equivalent of guru). They were nonconformists and original thinkers who believed that thought and practice had to come together.

In addition, Akbar spoke with Buddhists and Parsis (who had fled from Persia to western India to escape from the persecution of the Arab armies) in order to construct a religion that would integrate and represent the diversity of his vast empire. In 1578 CE he invited Jesuits to acquaint him with the gospels and allowed them to convert his people. He finally devised a syncretic religion derived from Islam, Hinduism, and Zoroastrianism, but the religion never prospered. Under his patronage, art and science flourished. He engaged historians to translate religious works into Persian, even supervising the translation of the *Mahabharata*.

Akbar is believed to have had many concubines, for he loved beauty and married many Rajput women to gain political strength. He dreamed of a united India. But he was not always a merciful victor. He demonstrated his ruthlessness during the conquest of the Rajput fortress of Chitor by ordering a massacre of thirty thousand Hindus. Many Rajput rulers had entered friendly alliances with Akbar. When Rana Uday Singh of Mewar refused to submit, Akbar lay siege to Chitor. While Uday Singh retired to the hills, the fort was left to the care of his generals. The fort quickly fell, every single soldier was killed, and the Rajput women immolated themselves. Akbar transformed the empire into a significant power. His rule marked the beginning of a new epoch in Indian history. His assertive personality, boundless energy, and political acumen were reproduced in a book of paintings with text called "Akbarnama," created by hundreds of court painters. It was completed during the early seventeenth century.

JEHANGIR

The children of Akbar could not hold the empire together after his death. His son Jehangir (ruled 1605–1627), born of a Turkish father and Hindu mother, was a strange mixture of tenderness and brutality, as well as justice and recklessness. His addiction to wine was his ruin. But he encouraged the arts, was an enthusiastic hunter, and constantly met with Hindu sages for debates and discussions on Hindu philosophy. His reign was a prosperous and opulent one remembered for its processions of silk-caparisoned elephants, its bejeweled nobles, and its exotic perfumes. Month-long festivities featured intoxicating drinks and dancing girls.

Although he had many women, Jehangir was deeply committed to his favorite wife, Nurjehan (Light of the World).

Nurjehan possessed a combination of beauty, brilliance, and ambition. She took charge of all imperial affairs because Jehangir indulged in pleasures, such as drinking innumerable cups of *arrack*, a local potent brew laced with opium, which distracted him from his duties as ruler. It is said Nurjehan once killed six tigers.

In 1622, Jehangir's son Shah Jehan attempted to seize the throne but failed. When Jehangir died, Shah Jehan came out of hiding, proclaimed himself emperor, and murdered his three brothers.

SHAH JEHAN AND THE TAJ MAHAL

A brutal, wasteful, and ruthless emperor, who ordered the killing of all his male relations who might possibly claim the throne, Shah Jehan (ruled 1627–1658 CE) also had a passion for architecture, and he imported Italian artists who taught his craftsmen the art of inlaying marble with a mosaic of precious stones. He built forts with luxurious halls bearing panels of Florentine mosaic on black marble, as well as ceilings and arches carved with such skill they looked like lace. However, he is mostly remembered for the hauntingly beautiful Taj Mahal, a tribute to his eternal love for his beauteous queen, Mumtaz Mahal (Exalted of the Palace). Mumtaz gave her husband fourteen children in eighteen years and died in childbirth at the age of thirty-nine.

In 1632 the mausoleum was built for the queen by the inconsolable Shah Jehan. There is no trace of Hindu influence. Artisans were brought from Baghdad, Constantinople, and other centers of the Muslim faith. It took twenty-two years and twenty-two thousand laborers and craftsmen from India, Asia, and Europe to build the white marble Taj. The building is set in a Persian landscaped garden on the banks of the Yamuna River. The Taj Mahal is exquisitely proportioned, with minarets and a central dome mirrored in a reflecting pool. It features perforated marble grilles, semiprecious stones (including jasper, lapis lazuli, and bloodstone) inlaid in marble, as well as arabesques and chevrons. There is hardly a break between the stones. One flower an inch square can have sixty different inlays. The Taj Mahal reflects the varying moods of night and day: brilliant and dazzling at noon, warm and glowing at dusk, and ethereal in the moonlight. The main entrance was once guarded with heavy silver gates. The stone carving is of alabaster lace, beautiful and sublime with delicate detail.

Another legendary work of art created at this time was the Peacock Throne, which took seven years to complete. It was legendary for its components of precious metals and stones. Four legs of gold supported the seat, and twelve pillars of emeralds held up the enameled canopy, while each pillar bore two peacocks glittering with rubies and pearls. Between the peacocks was a tree, covered with diamonds, emeralds, rubies, and pearls. The fabled throne was carried off to Persia in 1739 by Nadir Shah and then was gradually dismantled to pay off the expenses of the royal personages.

Yet another project on a grand scale, the Red Fort (Lal Kila)—of red sandstone—was built in Delhi in 1640. It includes towering ramparts, factories, storehouses, military barracks, stables, and a mint. It housed thousands of servants, courtiers, and princesses. A magnificent mosque, Jama Masjid, was built facing the main entrance. Every Friday, tens of thousands of Muslims in India still gather here to pray at noon.

Taj Mahal in Agra (courtesy of Robert Arnett, India Unveiled*).*

Jama Masjid mosque, Old Delhi (courtesy of Robert Arnett, India Unveiled).

Shah Jehan, the most lavish spender of the Moghul emperors, ruled for three decades. He began his reign by killing his brothers but neglected to kill his sons, one of whom, Aurangzeb, not only overthrew him but imprisoned him. Shah Jehan languished in prison for eight years, looking sorrowfully through a grille at his creation, the Taj Mahal, where the body of his beloved rested.

AURANGZEB AND THE MARATHAS

An orthodox Muslim, who read prayers at great length, fasted, and memorized the Koran, Aurangzeb (ruled 1658–1707 CE) was also a subtle diplomat. He soon set about an anti-Hindu policy, imposing Islam as he began his conquest of southern India. A Hindu religious sect, the Satnamis, were ruthlessly crushed, and in 1675 Tegh Bahadur, a leading Sikh guru, was executed because he refused to embrace Islam. The first Guru Nanak (1469–1538) had founded the Sikh faith, a balanced blend of Islam and Hinduism, after refusing to convert to Islam. But when the ninth guru was beheaded by Aurangzeb, the Sikhs unified into an Army of the Pure (Khalsa), forging militant Sikhism. The Sikhs, or disciples of Sikhism were religious reformers and had been attracting attention. During the eighteenth century, they became a ruling power.

Aurangzeb reintroduced the jizya (poll tax) for non-Muslims and new custom duties with a separate inflated rate for Hindus. He became unpopular, alienating and antagonizing the communities that Akbar had integrated. Aurangzeb ruled for forty-eight years, retaining his power right up to his death. He inspired terror and awe. It is said that his eldest son never received a letter from him without trembling in fear. He abhorred art, destroyed Hindu monuments, and smashed idols. In one year, sixty-six temples were broken in Amber alone, sixty-three at Chitor, and one hundred twenty-three at Udaipur.

A newborn power, the Marathas, rose from the rugged Western Ghats, an area that today is known as Maharashtra. Led by Shivaji Bhonsle (1627–1680), a Hindu leader and guerrilla tactician, the Marathas put up a formidable resistance to Aurangzeb's authority. Inhabiting the impregnable mountain ranges used as forts, the Marathas used these natural strongholds as a crucial element in their struggles against Aurangzeb. Shivaji, called the "mountain rat," who had begun his career as a small chieftain, organized a government on a Hindu pattern following the principles of Brahmin law. He made freedom his creed and fought tenaciously, armored by his ardent Hindu faith in his country. Illiterate and unable to even sign his name, he was well-versed in military and guerrilla strategies. Chivalrous and far-sighted, this Hindu leader's power rose to be a constant threat to the mighty Moghul Empire. The Maratha leaders came together and under the guidance of Shivaji instilled in their people political consciousness, patriotism, and devotion to the Hindu religion.

Once, in a daring exploit, Shivaji escaped from Agra, the stronghold of Aurangzeb, hidden in a basket of sweets. Disguised as a Hindu priest, he made his way back to the Deccan, where he continued his war with Aurangzeb. In June 1674, Shivaji was crowned Chatrapati, "the King," establishing a Hindu kingdom in the face of Muslim opposition. In the east, he claimed the territories of Nasik and Poona, as well as Vellore and Tanjore in the south. Although he lived in a cruel era, he made it a rule never to harm mosques, women, or the Koran. A champion of Hinduism and founder of the powerful Maratha Kingdom, Shivaji died at age fifty-three to be succeeded by his son Shambaji, who was captured, tortured, and put to death by Aurangzeb. Rajzram, another son of Shivaji, organized the Marathas once more to defeat the Moghuls. He died suddenly at the age of thirty and was succeeded by Tara Bai, his wife, who placed her four-year-old son on the throne. The Maratha Empire then continued under the Peshwas (Brahmin ministers).

DECLINE OF THE MOGHULS

At eighty-eight years of age, having ruled far too long, Aurangzeb awaited death. Some say he repented his excesses and cruelty on his deathbed. He realized that he had killed far too many and feared judgment.

Aurangzeb's reign had splintered the mighty Moghul Empire. The Marathas had established a state in the Western Ghats, the Rajputs were growing restless in the other parts of the subcontinent, and there was growing unrest in the Moghul Empire among Muslim subjects. The strain from constant wars, the exhaustion of the treasury, and internal conflict paved the way for the conquest of India by the British.

Aurangzeb left behind four sons who battled with one another. Finally, Prince Mauazzam, known as Bahadur Shah I, became the undisputed leader and made peace with the Rajputs.

- 9 -

Early European Voyages:
Leading to British Rule
(1500–1885 CE)

India had wisely established trade relations with Europe even in the early centuries of the Christian era. Western Europeans were seduced by the scent of spices and the enormous profits to be gained. Spices were needed to make meats rich in flavor and to make them last longer, as well as to mull wines and ales. In the fifteenth century, the Turkish Empire created a blockade in this lucrative trade. Thwarted, European traders tried to find alternative routes to India by charting a passage around Africa, crossing the Cape of Good Hope, and reaching the port of Calicut in Kerala.

THE PORTUGUESE

In 1498 the Portuguese sailor Vasco da Gama dropped anchor with his three little ships at Calicut—a fortuitous landing for him, as Calicut was renowned for spices, silks, sandalwood, and ivory. He sold the goods in Lisbon for an enormous profit, returned with twenty ships, and set up a warehouse at Cochin, trading in exotic commodities.

The Portuguese came not as conquerors but as colonizers. They were the first European power in India and based themselves with trading stations on the shores of Goa on the western coast of India. They enjoyed a lucrative monopoly and quickly set about Christianizing Indians with evangelical fervor. By the sixteenth century, the clergy wielded immense influence. Francis Xavier, a Spanish priest, was commissioned by the king of Portugal to go to India. On arriving in 1542, he saw a vast New World that appeared to be waiting to receive the Christian religion. He preached and ministered to the sick and went about converting thousands from Goa and South India, with zealous evangelism. His remains are enshrined in the Church of Bom Jesus in Goa.

But the power of the Portuguese declined due to various reasons.The primary cause was rebellion on the part of the people who were forced to embrace Christianity. Further, the discovery of Brazil distracted the Portuguese from their colonizing activities in India. Although they retained some territories in Goa till 1961, they were unable to compete with the next wave of European colonizers in India.

Because of its brief but powerful encounter with the Portuguese, Goa still retains a distinct identity with ostentatious baroque churches and Roman Catholicism.

THE DUTCH, DANES, AND FRENCH

In 1602, the Dutch set up trading ports in India near present-day Chennai (Madras) and then expanded all over the western coast and to Bengal. But they found it more profitable to trade for Indonesian spices and concentrated their energies in that country. In 1616 the Danes set up Protestant missions and a printing press in Serampore, Bengal. They, too, became diffident and sold Serampore to the British, who arrived in India at this time by sheer serendipity.

Following the examples of the Portuguese and Dutch, the French established a trading company in 1664 and set up factories in Surat and Masulipatnam. They founded the settlement of Pondicherry in 1674 in South India where even today some of the local Indians are fluent in French. In 1742 Joseph Dupleix came to India as governor of French possessions, and for a time the French and the East India Company fought for power over India. Meanwhile, France and Britain were at war over Austria's succession. Puppet Nawabs were installed with French advisors, and Dupleix tried to be the power behind the throne. But Versailles found him very expensive and arrogant, and he was recalled. The East India Company returned Pondicherry to the French, and the city became a district of France until it was ceded in 1954.

THE EAST INDIA COMPANY

The East India Company was inaugurated in September 1599 by a small group of London merchants who first sent ships to the Spice Islands of Java, Moluccas, and the lands east of the Cape of Good Hope. The East India Company could not get control of the lucrative spice trade on the islands of Indonesia, which was controlled by the Dutch, and so was lured to India on hearing of its valuable spices, silks, and jewels. The company arrived in India in 1608 with the blessing of Queen Elizabeth I to trade profitably and peacefully. Cheap labor also was exploited. The company thwarted both French and Portuguese trade in India, setting up a chain of factories all around the country with the most important being Madras (Chennai) and Calcutta. In 1668, the company picked up

Bombay (Mumbai), for ten pounds, when Charles II made a gift of Bombay, which had been part of his dowry from his Portuguese wife, Catherine of Braganza.

The company traded silver and firearms in return for silk, cotton, indigo, opium, jewels, and spices. The East India Company was the largest company in Britain with dockyards, warehouses, and sawmills. But it still had no intention of conquering India. The trading posts had to be defended with soldiers since they were situated in a land disturbed with internal rivalries. These outposts expanded into small cities, and the outposts became the stamping grounds for small armies. By the middle of the eighteenth century the company was a serious force, and the turbulent Moghul Empire began to disintegrate. The East India Company's trade in cotton, yarn, and indigo accelerated, and they became firmly entrenched through much manipulation, exploitation, and plundering. Returning to England, company officers bought up seats in Parliament and sprawling country homes. Tales of luxurious living attracted scores of young British men and their women to India. Calcutta (Kolkatha) in Bengal became the center of operations.

Each city had its own ghetto, with Europeans enclosed in one part of the town and the merchants and locals in another. Many of the English arrived in India in their teens, working as clerks. It is said they indulged in gambling, drinking, fifteen-course dinners, luxurious mansions, servants, and hookahs often loaded with opium. But the British also had to confront the heat and the dust, jungle fever, cholera, malaria, and smallpox. Bombay became known as the "burying ground" of the British, and Calcutta was often called Golgotha, or the "place of skulls."

Gateway of India, Mumbai.

The English continued to misuse their trade privileges and were said to have instigated the Hindus against Muslim rulers. In 1756, Siraj-ud-Daulah, the ruling Nawab of Bengal, believed Calcutta to be richer than it really was and resolved to loot the place and drive out the English. Leading thirty thousand foot soldiers, four hundred trained elephants, and twenty thousand horsemen, the Nawab seized the British settlement in Calcutta. He reputedly confined and suffocated one hundred forty-six people in an airless eighteen- by fourteen-foot chamber, which historians later called the Black Hole of Calcutta. The English were stunned and outraged. Stories of English soldiers sucking sweat off their shirts and other victims drinking their own tears inflamed the rage of the British, and they were ready for revenge.

Robert Clive led British soldiers and a few thousand Indians to defeat the twenty-one-year-old Nawab's army on the battlefield of Plassey and wreak vengeance. Historians believe that the battle was won through the treachery of the Nawab's uncle, who was bribed by the British to hold back the Indian cavalry. With two thousand native soldiers (*sepoys*) and eight hundred British troops, Clive recaptured the province of Bengal and restored trading privileges. The Battle of Plassey was a turning point in the British conquest of India, making them the governors of Bengal from where they ruled India. The enfeebled and powerless Moghul emperor made Clive the revenue collector (*diwan*) for the whole state of Bengal.

Another significant event that contributed to making the British a sovereign power in India was the hard-fought Battle of Buxar in 1764 in which the English delivered a crushing defeat to a group of Indian princes, including the Moghul emperor. This victory made Clive governor of Bengal again. A man of iron will, dauntless courage, and determination, Clive was the founder of the British Empire. There are many stories of shameless British plunder during Clive's "reign"—of ransoms demanded, extortion from the Nabobs (local princes), and beheadings of those who rebelled. The Parliament in Britain was shocked at the atrocities, and they started inquiries asking for periodic reviews. Clive was recalled. He returned to England in 1767, where he committed suicide

Like Clive, Warren Hastings joined the East India Company as a clerk in 1750. He was an educated man who studied Bengali and Persian. He was a strict disciplinarian who took cold baths, rode eight miles each day before breakfast, and was in bed by ten at night. His extraordinary intelligence and perseverance made him governor general of Bengal. He was later removed from office for his unjust and rapacious decisions in the Rohilla war. He foolishly took part in this conflict to help the Nawab of Oudh, a British ally, against people who had given no offense to the English. Other charges against Hastings included the execution of his longstanding enemy, Nand Kumar, who was an influential Brahmin of Bengal, on a trumped-up forgery case. He was also accused of extorting large sums of money and jewelry from the Begums of Oudh. But he is remembered for his diplomatic triumph when a French fleet arrived in the Bay of Bengal, threatening repercussions. He also had to contend with Haider Ali of Mysore, the Nizam of Hyderabad, and the Maratha confederacy, as well as the Moghul emperor. In his own manipulative way, he managed to integrate British India. Despite being accused of serious crimes, he was finally acquitted.

Lord Cornwallis (1786–1798) replaced Hastings and established the beginnings of a civil service with all high positions reserved for the British. Private ownership of land in Bengal was introduced under his regulation code. Intermediaries who did liaison work between the monarch and the peasant were now given property and became landlords (*zamindars*) for a price that included funds to maintain the company Raj. The Indians paid for the upkeep of their new rulers through this permanently fixed sum of revenue. When there was monsoon failure, the zamindars lost their lands as they had used their deeds to secure loans. The growing use of English in Bengal, Madras, and Bombay was another social agent of change during this time.

Lord Wellesley (1798–1805) became governor general and was determined to subdue all Indian aggressors. The state of Mysore had risen to prominence through the drive of its energetic founder, Haider Ali (1761–1782), who was a powerful threat to the British. He was succeeded by his son, Tipu Sultan, a brave Muslim soldier, who constantly tried to outthink and outmaneuver the British. Tippu Sultan was finally killed by the English in his capital, Sriringapattanam, in 1799. There had been major clashes between the rulers of Mysore and Hyderabad. Tipu Sultan was the most aggressive enemy in Mysore, but even he was overthrown and Mysore was annexed. Soon the princes and rulers of Indian states were guaranteed security by installing a contingent of British troops at their own expense. In truth, the Indian rulers and others were forced to agree to these payments. The lust for power grew with the British advancing easily into central India.

Opposing Forces and Reforms

At about the same time, an aggressive dynasty was founded in Burma (1752–1760). The following years saw the Burmese rapidly extending their territories into Assam and Manipur, and they succeeded in gaining parts of Bengal. The British, led by Governor General Lord Amherst, decided to attack by sea and sent a powerful naval fleet. This proved unsuccessful at first, but eventually the British regained their supremacy, the Burmese were quelled, and the northeastern frontier of India was once again protected against foreign aggression.

During the period of 1802–1819, the powerful Marathas were one of the strongest forces in India that opposed the British. But they, too, were riddled with warring factions. Through their infamous divide and rule policy, the British created splits among them. Establishing a covert spy network, the British infiltrated the Afghans and North Indian Muslims to instigate war with the Marathas, so that the Marathas would be forced to ask for British protection. The British triumphed, and the Marathas capitulated.

The Sikhs in northern India who dominated Punjab were also a formidable force, but after many brutal, bloody battles they were subdued, and the British conquered Lahore, the capital of the Sikh empire. It was during this period that the famous Kohinoor diamond (Mountain of Light) was taken away from Maharaja Duleep Singh who signed away his kingdom as well as the diamond to Britain's Queen Victoria to adorn her crown. After one more bloodthirsty war in 1849, the British gained control of the north, southeast, and west of India. Good timing and tenacity helped them. Territories were annexed outright, treaties guaranteed British autonomy, the Indian nobility was forced to become subservient and act as British proxies, and confederacies were divided. Victorious campaigns were the order of the day. Indian disunity and military inefficiency, as well as the eagerness of many Indians to serve the British rather than native rulers, accounted for the rapid expansion of the British Empire.

Lord William Bentinck's arrival (ruled 1828–1835) brought in its wake many significant reforms. The most famous reform associated with this period is the abolition of sati in 1829. Relatives often urged widows to perform sati stating that the widow should join her God-husband. The practice was also induced by the family who looked for the prestige of a sati in the family. Property also could be claimed by the remaining relatives, and then they could relinquish the responsibility of taking care of and feeding a single woman whom no one would marry. Burning or burying of widows of Hindus became illegal and punishable by criminal courts. Another social reform banned *thuggee*, the practice of armed gangs strangling wayfarers. Thousands of thuggees were arrested and punished. Lord Bentinck also threw open the doors for Indians to official employment in the judicial and executive areas. The English language became the literary and official language of the country, as well as the vehicle for higher education. Lord Dalhousie (1848–1856), a brilliant Scottish nobleman and the next governor general, initiated an ambitious program of modernization with sweeping reforms. English education spread, and three universities were founded in Madras, Bombay, and Calcutta.

However, the energetic Dalhousie came up with a new policy through which the Hindu law that recognized the right of an Indian ruler to adopt his heir was terminated. Instead, the British insisted that if the ruler did not have a natural heir, the British would annex the state. By this method, many independent states came under the control of the British. Dalhousie founded the Post and Telegraph Department and also introduced the electric telegraph. He determined that railways would connect the nation and was able to open a short line in 1853. Under his supervision, roads and irrigation systems were designed and Indian-language schools were opened in all districts.

Meanwhile, in Burma, the king again declared war on British subjects. In April 1852, Rangoon, the Burmese capital, was captured by the British. The annexation of Burmese territory isolated the country.

Just north of India, although a predominantly Muslim area, Kashmir, a beauteous, fertile land was ruled by a Sikh, Ranjit Singh. It fell into the hands of the British due to misrule. Under the treaty of Amritsar, the British then sold Kashmir to the highest bidder—Gulab Singh, a Hindu—for a paltry sum. This brought about a series of uprisings against Hindu rulers by the majority of Muslims in Kashmir.

In 1858, the East India Company ceased to be a trading company, although it still had shareholders and directors. Instead, the Crown assumed rule of India and the Company.

~ 10 ~
The British Raj:
From Trade to Dominion

The power and the glory of British rule in India came to be known as the Raj, and India was the most sparkling and glittering jewel in the crown of the British Colonial Empire. The lore, mystique, history, romance, and glamour of the British Raj have inspired countless books, films, and plays.

The dramatic expansion of British power over the vast Indian Empire was systematically established by implementing covert operations and exploiting political divisions. Indian rulers were given security instead of responsibility. Those Indians who aspired to attain high positions were encouraged to go to England to pass the exams. This deterred many, resulting in Indians' stagnating at subordinate level in the railways, technical services, and public works. British power clamped down tightly on Indian ambition, while missionaries arrived to reveal Christianity to the "heathen." Mission schools and hospitals were set up, and many Indians converted, although it was evident that most of them were from the oppressed castes. But the missionaries also were responsible for encouraging the study of Indian languages, and the Bible was quickly printed in Bengali, Hindi, Tamil, Telugu, and Marathi. Grammar books and dictionaries in local languages flourished. Self-confident and conspicuously aware of their superiority over their Indian subjects, the British had already made English the official language of business and education.

As a result, a new breed of Indians evolved, and as Lord Macaulay, the historian (1850–1909), put it succinctly, it was "a class of persons Indian in blood and color, but English in taste, in opinions, in morals, and intellects." An elite group thus emerged, one that spoke and studied English in India and Europe. Speech clearly demarcated those who had no access to English education.

The next wave of British colonists from England were educated people who loved plays, ritualistic dinner parties, balls, social calls, fireworks, and picnics. Some rode in carriages with embroidered curtains. A captain usually had a retinue of a cook, a valet, a housekeeper, a grass cutter, a barber, a laundryman, a steward, and, in many cases, a mistress. He also had coolies (laborers) to transport his bed, campstools, trunks of tableware, bottles of wine, live poultry, and a tent for supplies.

The next one hundred and fifty years saw sweeping reforms and Westernization, including the spread of education by the foundation of schools and universities, as well as museums and libraries. Laws regulating inheritance, divorce, marriage, and laws of contracts were uniformly applied to all citizens of India. No one could be detained without a trial.

Delhi, was inaugurated in 1911 as the new capital; today Delhi still houses the government and is the residence of the president of India.

Indian rituals, customs, and observances were regarded as primitive and idolatrous. Victorian prudishness scorned

Indian culture as stagnant and backward. However, one of the positive aspects of the Raj in India was demonstrated by the prohibition of sati in 1829. Many Indians hailed this as a humane action, but others contended it was an attack on Indian culture and the freedom of choice of the bereaved widow. Another reform that benefited women was the Hindu Widow Act of 1856, permitting widows to remarry, which was otherwise forbidden by Hindu law.

Lord Dalhousie oversaw a broad program of modernization that included the introduction of an efficient economical postal service and railways. This regime saw the first three hundred miles of railway track laid in India—the British little realizing they were laying the foundations of what would become the largest passenger train service in the world. On April 16, 1853, when the carriages rolled onto the tracks of Bombay (Mumbai), there was a twenty-one gun salute, and a public holiday was declared. Today, twelve thousand trains hurtle to seven thousand destinations spread over thirty-nine thousand miles of hills, valleys, and plains.

Writers and observers of the history of the Indian railways have also noted and regretted that the Indian laborers who worked the tracks suffered greatly. Some four thousand workers died in a single cholera epidemic while working on the East India Railway. The Industrial Revolution was sweeping through England and ironically brought about significant changes in the economy of India. Cotton cloth manufactured in Manchester mills was sold in India, putting the spinners and weavers of India out of work. There were no duties on British imports, and millions of craftsmen were forced to go back to the land and depend on the soil rather than their creative skills. England produced finished goods and ruined India's textile industry, forcing farmers to raise cash crops needed for the British machines. Britain excluded the rest of the world from the Indian market, forcing their textiles on India, and they taxed Indian textiles destined for England. At the same time, the British insidiously set up their own caste system with well-bred officers in their conclave and ordinary soldiers and natives who kept themselves in what was known as the Black Town. British civilian and army officers drew enormous salaries, and Indian papers and journals were published under heavy censorship. Meanwhile, there were instances of apartheid with exclusive British clubs, tyranny of martial law in certain provinces, and notices that read, "No dogs and Indians allowed."

Indians were becoming alarmed at the growing power of the British Empire, and this fear was shared by Hindus who believed that Indian religion and culture were in danger of being compromised. The East India Company's army was made up of two hundred thousand Indian troops (sepoys) and ten thousand British officers. This was a dangerous situation for the British. Soon outbreaks of discontent became rampant. Finally in 1857, when a new Enfield rifle was issued with cartridges greased not with wax and vegetable oil, but with cow and pig fat (the end of each cartridge had to be bitten off before it could be loaded), the sepoys of Bengal revolted. No Hindu would touch cow fat, and pig fat was forbidden for Muslims. It is believed that the British were sensitive to these traditions, and orders may have gotten confused. Eighty-five sepoys in Meerut refused to use the new cartridges and were thrown into jail. The rest of the sepoys of Bengal, one whole division, slaughtered every Britisher they could find in Delhi. The

Mutiny of 1857 spread across northern and central India. The British were butchered in many a city, and towns became rubble. The British retaliated by bayoneting every sepoy in sight and conducting mass hangings. Indian soldiers became confused about their leadership, with many loyal retainers protecting British women and children, some faithful sepoy regiments sacrificing their lives for the rulers, and some Indian princely states remaining loyal toward the British.

The British returned to power with a vengeance. Rape, pillage, and murder were the war cries heard in many a city. When the outraged British recaptured their losses, India was swamped with blood and carnage. In Madhya Pradesh, the Rani of Jhansi, Lakshmi Bai, is remembered as the leader of a rebellion that killed all Britishers and their families. The Rani died fighting, dressed like a man, and if the legend is true, using her sword with both hands and holding the reins of the horse in her mouth. Poets, dramatists, and historians have eulogized the twenty-two-year old Lakshmi Bai, who died in 1858. In a popular Indian ballad she is described as a heroine fighting like a tigress. She inspired courage and even encouraged women to join the army and take a more active role in India's independence.

When the mutiny was eventually crushed, evaluation procedures were launched and British policies toward India were scrutinized. The East India Company was taken over by the Crown. New guidelines stipulated that Indian customs and religions were to be left strictly alone. New treaties were drawn, and five hundred forty-two Indian princely states were established, which were semi-independent and self-governing. The number of Indian army officers was scaled down, and artillery was kept in British hands. High courts were established in the larger cities. Indians were deliberately excluded from holding high positions as the British had become deeply suspicious and trusted no Indian.

British cantonments emerged. These self-contained communities offered a separate British world with markets, churches, hospitals, bungalows, and even jails. Hill stations in the cool verdant hills became famous landmarks, including Simla in Himachal Pradesh and Ootacamund in the south. Even now, these communities contain quaint and charming gabled cottages, as well as streets named after Britishers.

In 1911 George V, Queen Victoria's grandson, became the king and emperor of Delhi. The British struggled valiantly to keep Britain alive in the turbulence of India. They planted English flowers in their gardens, covered their furniture with chintz, served elaborate English teas, and ordered patterns for dressmaking from across the seas. Cheap labor helped to amuse the British in India, who indulged excessively in sports, picnics, dances, and parties. But the discomforts of hot and humid weather, tropical diseases, mosquitoes, sullen servants, and boredom began to take their toll.

The missionaries converted many, ran schools for Indian girls, did medical work, and started orphanages.

Some British women married Indians. Others found in India something that satisfied their restless souls. Sister Nivedita, born Margaret Noble, came from a religious and poor family. She became a teacher, then a journalist and a socialist. After hearing lectures by reformer Swami Vivekananda (spiritual teacher of Hindu philosophy) in London, she journeyed to India in 1891, studied Bengali, and entered his order in Calcutta. Her writings took on a political turn as she denounced

British rule, became involved with Indian nationalism, and was even imprisoned. On her release, Congress elected Sister Nivedita as president. But Mahatma Gandhi was spearheading nationalism, and Nivedita reconciled herself to being a low-profile social worker.

Mahatma Gandhi (courtesy of Consulate of India, San Francisco).

The Indian Nationalist Movement: The Road to Freedom and Democracy

(1885 CE–Present)

The Indian National Congress was formed in 1885 to establish national unity and seek economic freedom from the British. A growing political awakening was in its nascent stage. A new breed of educated upper- and middle-class Indians who were teachers, scholars, reformers, philosophers, journalists, and lawyers initiated a nationalist movement. At first, the movement was concentrated only among the educated Indians, but the leaders soon realized that for a free India, grassroots energy had to be spread through the vernacular Indian languages across the masses of the Indian population. By 1907 two prominent groups emerged: one moderate under Gopal Krishna Ghokale, and the other extremist under Bal Gangadhar Tilak, who sought *swaraj* (self-rule).

THE REVIVAL OF HINDUISM

Hinduism was revived with fervor and invigorated by a brilliant intellectual, Ram Mohan Roy (1772–1883). He condemned the caste system and tried to rid Hinduism of negative customs like child marriage and other social taboos. Roy mastered Greek, Latin, Persian, Sanskrit, and Arabic. Along with others, he launched newspapers and cultural societies reinforcing traditional Hindu and nationalist ideas and attacking the abuse of the caste system. He founded the Brahmo Samaj in 1828 and denounced infanticide and political bigotry, polygamy, and idolatry.

A new generation realized that Hindu culture had much of permanent value and there was no need to slavishly follow the West in order to solve problems. The Arya Samaj was one such organization that reformed Hinduism of its negativity and returned to the Vedas. Europeans and Americans became aware of the depth of Indian religion through the Ramakrishna Mission, the Theosophical Society, and Swami Vivekananda. Hinduism was studied in the West with the accent on social action through religion.

In the ferment of widespread reform and revival of Hindu nationalism, both Hindu reformers and the British banned the devadasi tradition in which women were dedicated to the temples to dance and sing in honor of the residing deity. This tradition had existed in India for centuries before the arrival of the British. The devadasi was considered to be the Nitya-sumangali (the evergreen bride), on account of her symbolic marriage to the God who was not a mortal and thereby never could die and leave her a widow. According to Hindu law, the devadasi was able to lead a progressive lifestyle, compared to other women. A devadasi could possess property, live without a man, and have children out of wedlock. The Victorian British and extreme and conservative Hindus banned the dance under the Anti Nautch Act (*nautch* is the anglicized corruption of the word *naach,* which is "to dance" in Urdu).

In 1905, Lord Curzon divided Bengal into two distinct halves—Hindu versus Muslim communities—on the pretext

that it was too unwieldy to manage. In reality, this was a bla-
tant strategy to check the rapidly growing strength of the
Indian community by increasing tensions between Hindus
and Muslims. In 1906 the Muslim League was formed. Congress drew the multitudes of Indians together and retaliated
against the partition through a boycott of British goods,
through protests, and through demonstrations with the chants
of "swaraj" and "swadeshi" (one's own country).

In Amritsar in 1919, a British force opened fire on an Indian
meeting in a walled area called Jallianwalabagh. Four hundred
Indians were killed, and one thousand were wounded. The massacre at Jallianwallabagh was hailed as a triumph of the British,
and General Dyer, the officer in command, was declared a hero.
Shocked by this callousness and brutality, many loyal Indian
supporters of the Raj embraced nationalism.

Meanwhile, during the First World War in 1914, Indians
showed their loyalty to the British rulers by fighting in France
and the Middle East. Sixty thousand were killed, and India
hoped to be rewarded. After all, Australia and Canada had been
granted self-government by the British. Instead, the British
crushed any sign of dissent, political or otherwise.

MAHATMA GANDHI

The horrific outrage in Jallianwallabagh had a deep and profound effect on Mohandas Karamchand Gandhi (1869–1948),
who came to be known as the Father of the Indian Nation, or
the Mahatma (Great Soul). Born into a prosperous family at
Porbundar, a princely state in western India, he married at
thirteen, became a father at eighteen, and went off to England

to become a lawyer. He took lessons in elocution and ballroom dancing but became more conscious of his Indian heritage, history, and culture. He read the Bible, the *Bhagvad Gita*, and the teachings of Buddha. He then was engaged by a Muslim firm to represent its interests in cases in South Africa.

It was in South Africa that Gandhi encountered the horrific discrimination meted out by white racists. He was once thrown out of a first class railway carriage because of his skin color. He organized the Indian Natal Congress and advocated nonviolent resistance. He and his supporters were imprisoned for their revolutionary tactics to strike against hatred and discrimination in South Africa.

In 1915, Gandhi returned to India to participate in the growing unrest against the British Empire. He soon found himself abandoning European dress to wear instead the traditional *dhoti* (lower garment) and sandals of the peasants of India. Identifying with the untouchables, Gandhi traveled third class across India to learn about the nation and its people, teaching inner soul force (*satyagraha*), nonviolence, and self-control. Hatred was irrational, he said, and violence was to be suppressed. In his autobiography, *The Story of My Experiments with Truth*, he decried the practice of untouchability and dreamt of a utopia of self-contained village republics where people would live simple lives in small, self-sustaining neighborhoods, cooking their own food and spinning yarn while reducing their needs to the minimum. In this vision, the frail Gandhi intelligently integrated Hinduism and European philosophy and Satyagraha, which embodied love, peace, and self-discipline.

A dynamic pacifist, worshipped by millions as a Mahatma (Great Soul), Gandhi responded to British rule with his homespun philosophies of noncooperation and mass civil disobedience. Gandhi invented the "Quit India" slogan, which demanded

British withdrawal from the country. The weapons that the Mahatma wielded included hunger strikes (or *hartal*), boycotts of foreign materials, suspension of business, and the refusal to pay taxes. He advocated the power of meditation and abstinence. Self-purification demanded purification in all walks of life. To attain purity, one had to be free of passion in thought, speech, and action. Gandhi regarded untouchability as the greatest sin, and he gave the untouchables a new name, *Harijan* (children of God). He often washed the feet of the Harijan and brought seventy million of them into the mainstream of Indian life.

He attacked child marriage and championed women's equality. Many Indian women joined Gandhi's movement. Democracy to Gandhi was characterized by equal regard for all religions, opposition to untouchability, dignity of labor, and concern for the poor. The Brahmins found themselves isolated as Gandhi preached about love for the outcaste and wrote stirring articles on ethics, religion, untouchability, and nonviolence. He believed in the principle that each man is his brother's keeper. Through the power of love he wished to win over aggressors and resolve conflicts. Imprisoned several times, Gandhi continued to challenge the British with ahimsa (nonviolence) and satyagraha. His shaven head and sparse clothing fascinated the twentieth century. He lived frugally and fasted frequently. The world and the British saw him as an imposter, a fanatic, an astute politician, or a curiosity.

Meanwhile, the Indian Nationalist Movement gathered momentum and support from Indians of all religions and walks of life. The demand for women's rights became more vociferous, and women found themselves involved in intense politics and public life. Sarojini Naidu, a poet and activist, was a prominent member of the Congress Committee, and Vijay-lakshmi Pandit, a sister of political leader Jawarharlal Nehru, was a minister in the first Congress cabinet.

In 1930, on the Salt March, Gandhi and seventy-eight of his followers marched to the sea to protest against the British tax on salt. The march was a two-hundred-mile walk for twenty-nine days, from Ahmedabad to Dandi. On reaching the coast, Gandhi proceeded to make salt from seawater, in symbolic defiance of the British monopoly on salt. The march drew the attention of the world to the Indian independence movement. Gandhi was imprisoned.

The *charka* (spinning wheel) was used by Gandhi to demonstrate India's self-reliance. The British had stifled India's textile industry, and the hand-spun *khadi* (cotton) represented self-sufficiency and nationalism. Spinning wheels long displaced by the British mills were back on track. Gandhi insisted the nation return to indigenously manufactured goods. Many vowed to wear only khadi. Today there is an amazing range of khadi products: saris, bed quilts, shirts, and floor rugs in a variety of textures and colors. The khadi industry provides employment to millions of villages. Every village has its own khadi institution. With such campaigns, the nationalist cause and the Congress attracted not only the elite but also the farmers, factory workers, and laborers. Nationalism became a powerful mass movement cutting across all cultures and religions.

The agitators paid a price, however. Thousands of Indians were imprisoned, and hundreds were killed or injured in spite of their peaceful demonstrations against the British. But the strategy worked, and the British soon realized that they could not control India in the face of mass opposition.

Meanwhile, Indians were making a significant name for themselves on the world stage. From 1928 to 1960 the Indian hockey team won six gold medals and philosopher S. V. Radhakrishnan was acclaimed for his work. Rabindranath Tagore contributed poetry, prose, drama, and song and revitalized Bengali literature. He was awarded the Nobel Prize for Literature in 1913. Tagore started painting when he was sixty-seven, and by the age of eighty-one he had painted nearly two thousand pictures in ink and gouache, transferring the rhythmic quality of his verse into graphic designs. His poems radiated a spirit of humanism, symbolizing the intellectual ferment in Bengal.

For the first time, India became completely united under the auspices of British imperialism. Appointed by Gandhi, Jawaharlal Nehru (1889–1964), a dynamic and charismatic politician and a radical young thinker, became the leader of the Congress movement, while the Gandhian movement also inspired radical and articulate Subhas Chandra Bose and Vallabhai Patel. A realist from Gujarat, Patel leaned toward orthodoxy and authoritarianism. Subhas Bose from Bengal, however, was disillusioned with the civil disobedience movement and might have been responsible for an antigovernment movement, but Gandhi skillfully isolated him and chose Nehru as his successor. Nehru had great political acumen, apart from a refined education and good looks. He was a brilliant, insightful writer and produced two classic works, *Autobiography* and *Discovery of India.*

Nehru's greatest rival was Muhammad Ali Jinnah, an erudite, elegant, articulate politician and Muslim lawyer from the All India Muslim League. Jinnah had become disenchanted with the Congress and was interested in bringing together a cohesive group representing eighty million Muslims. An increasing number of Muslims began to join the Muslim League in response to the Hindu majority in the Congress. The Muslims were constantly encountering overwhelming Hindu presence, whether it was the Congress flag with Gandhi's famous charka flying from every public building, or the Hindu hymn of liberty, "Vande Mataram," which was sung in classrooms, on the streets, on the radio, and in homes. The notion that Hindustan belonged only to the Hindus became a breeding ground for dissension. The Muslims also had little inclination to merge with the Hindus as the religion differed radically. Hindus worshipped idols and the cow and adhered to the caste system. Muslims did not believe in reincarnation or karma. Islam had to reach into the core of its religion for nourishment and renewal. Islam had to safeguard itself and be distinct from Hinduism and not accept majority rule, which in short was Hindu rule. There was a sense of urgency among the Muslims as they looked toward Jinnah for guidance. Jinnah took over the Muslim League and hoped for a coalition with the Congress. But Congress won majorities in many provinces and declined a coalition. Jinnah was stunned and was not prepared to accept a minority position in India. He was made intensely aware of a deep sense of alienation and separateness. He was now determined to preach the doctrine of national independence and the two separate nations theory. Pakistan "Land of the Pure" (a word coined by Muslim academicians in Oxford) began to take visible shape.

The Congress had hoped to represent all religions and was disheartened by the growing strength of the Muslim League as an oppositional force. Jinnah envisioned a separate land for Muslims. Later he would become the founder of Pakistan.

India's Independence and Hindu–Muslim Partition

India had taken part decisively in the First and Second World Wars of 1914 and 1939. Princes had offered their treasuries, and some thousands of Indian troops were deployed. Indians were asked to fight Hitler and save democracy while they were denied self-government. The irony did not escape the British, who were slowly recognizing their responsibility to India. In fact, Sir Lord William Bentinck, governor general of India, had said as early as 1804 that if Britain was to be great, it had to be founded on the rock of peace and happiness in India. Twenty years later, Thomas Munroe said that the British regime ultimately wanted Indians to govern and protect themselves. No longer dealing with separate individual princes and states, the British were now confronting the massive nation of a unified India with a common goal, "Freedom from the Raj." After the Second World War, the British government supported the initiation of the Indian constitution drawn up by Indians in 1935. But who would rule India after the British left?

While India was steadily progressing forward on the path of self-government by Indians for Indians, at the same time it was supremely conscious of Jinnah's desire for a separate state. Jinnah believed that Hindus and Muslims could not coexist. Over the years, the British had strategically pitted the Muslims against the Hindus, supporting the All India Muslim League and encouraging the notion that Muslims were a distinct political community. Throughout British India, separate electorates had been offered to the Muslims, underscoring their separateness from Hindus and sowing the seeds of communalism. The Morley–Minto reforms in 1908 had allowed direct election for seats and separate or communal representation for Muslims.

This was the harbinger for the formation of the Muslim League in 1906. In 1940, the Muslim League, representing one-fifth of the total population of India, became a unifying force. They were resentful that they were not sufficiently represented in Congress and feared for the safety of Islam.

The British decided that the only way to solve the issue was to allow Jinnah his separate state. Prime Minister Attlee of Britain sent out a new viceroy, Lord Mountbatten (1946–1947), who promptly pressured India into a land of divided rule. The plan was to separate northwest India and eastern Bengal where Muslims were most numerous. This would become Jinnah's Pakistan. This decision was not only historic but also a terrible tragedy in the history of both India and Pakistan. The consequences of the partition have been devastating for both nations.

At midnight on August 15, 1947, India became independent. One day earlier, in Karachi, Jinnah had become the first governor general of the New Republic of Islamic Pakistan. In India at that auspicious hour, Jawaharlal Nehru proclaimed that "long years ago we made a tryst with destiny, and now the time comes when we shall redeem our pledge not wholly or in full measure, but very substantially. At the stroke of the midnight hour, when the world sleeps, India will awake to life and freedom. A moment comes, which comes but rarely in history, when we slip out from the old to the new, when an age ends, and when the soul of a nation long suppressed finds utterance." (All India Radio broadcast.)

But there was to be no peace. Instead, the most brutal and bloody events took place. Partition had horrifying consequences. Hindus and Sikhs moved out of Pakistan, while Muslims fled westward from India. Five million refugees moved, crisscrossing one another. In this scenario, tensions were escalated, and horrifying bloodbaths resulted as train-loads of refugees were massacred. Half a million people are thought to have lost their lives. It was one of the great human catastrophes of history. People exchanged countries and homes overnight, while all around there was slaughter, rape, savagery, and brutality. Refugees traveled in cars, buses, and trains or on foot with lines stretching hundreds of miles. Stories of bit-terness, hate, and rage still affect the cruel and bloody memo-ries of the brutal politics that divided India between Hindus and Muslims.

Gandhi was horrified and deeply shattered by the parti-tion of India and Pakistan. He had fought hard to sustain and encourage Hindu–Muslim relations. Gandhi often said that death for him would be a glorious deliverance, rather than that he should be a helpless witness to the destruction of India, Hin-duism, Sikhism, and Islam. He resided in a Muslim area in Delhi and promised to fast until his death. This quiet threat calmed the nation; however, many Hindus blamed Gandhi for supporting the Muslims. He was called "Mohammad Gandhi" because he often quoted prayers from the Koran.

In 1948, Gandhi was assassinated during a prayer meeting. A thirty-five-year-old Hindu man, Nathuram Godse, approached Gandhi and fired a single bullet. Gandhi died with the words "Hey Ram" (Oh God) on his lips. This was a heartbreakingly vio-lent ending to a man who did not believe in taking "an eye for an eye," for he firmly believed that this would render the whole world blind.

When Gandhi died, Jawaharlal Nehru, who had the gift of choosing the apt word, broke the news to the people in a broad-cast over All India Radio. In ringing words he said, "The light has gone out of our lives and there is darkness everywhere. . . .

The light that shone in this country was no ordinary light. The light that has illumined this country for so many years will illumine this country for many more years, and a thousand years later that light will still be seen in this country, and the world will see it, and it will give solace to innumerable hearts." (All India Radio broadcast.)

THE NEHRU DYNASTY

When the British left, India was a multireligious, multiregional, multiethnic country, exploited, backward, and poor from colonialism. Imitating a Soviet-style system of centralization and economic planning, Nehru launched a socialist experiment in India, closing the country to international trade and placing tariffs on foreign goods. He impeded India's economic development with protectionism and domestic regulation and enforced controls on production, prices, and employment. This resulted in a misguided focus on capital goods, which led to badly managed state-run enterprise, corruption, and widespread poverty. His daughter, Indira Gandhi, revised Nehru's neglect of agriculture for industrialization and was later responsible for the Green Revolution in an attempt to abolish poverty and make India self-sufficient in food. Still, deprivation continued to encompass the landscape, and socialism was a burden.

Finally, her son Rajiv Gandhi attempted to initiate economic liberalization, desiring freedom from Nehru's inheritance. For forty years, the economy had grown slowly due to colonialism and the horrors of partition, poverty, caste, and corruption. The need for a new direction was evident. Answers were found in the beginning of liberalization. The

Indian government began to find opportunities in the international community and with startlingly triumphant reforms in 1991–1993, India opened its doors to free trade with a liberal budget, tax cuts, and deregulation. Finally, democracy began to renew and reinvent India, increasing stability and serving the cause of economic freedom.

A high-caste Brahmin, Jawaharlal Nehru, educated at Harvard, was the first prime minister of India, serving from 1947 to 1964. Mahatma Gandhi had made a deep and lasting impression on Nehru. A staunch believer in social reform and justice, Nehru abhorred Hindu orthodoxy and casteism. He supported equal rights for all and was a democrat to the core, even though he admired the Communist Soviet Union. His strong commitment to the vital foundation of democracy helped India to achieve an economic transformation without coercion and the loss of freedom. Known as Panditji (teacher), Nehru's brilliant intellect, unflinching patriotism, and attempts to eradicate poverty made him perhaps the greatest Indian leader after Gandhi.

India was now the world's largest democracy. Nehru's Congress Party won three hundred sixty-four of the four hundred ninety-nine seats in the Lok Sabha, guaranteeing the people's confidence in Nehru and the party. The Communists were confined to Kerala, which was the only state to hold out against the Congress Party sweep. Other parties, like the orthodox Swatantara and the capitalist Jan Sangh, tried to drum up support based on Hindu chauvinism. Soon each state demanded complete independence, and the Indian map became fragmented according to languages (Tamil, Telugu, Kannada, Punjabi, Malayalam, Gujarati, Assamese, and others) spoken by different communities. Much against Nehru's desire and despite his vision of a united country, Andhra Pradesh became the first linguistic state in south India in 1956.

Nehru realized the most critical and urgent issue facing India was poverty. He collaborated with industrialists like J. R. D. Tata and set up socialist Five-year Plans. Established industries were controlled by private enterprises, and public ventures were taken over by the state. Nehru yearned for India to be able to produce all its own food, power, and steel. He wanted to free India from dependency on overseas supplies. National independence was his creed, as well as noninvolvement in foreign affairs. This view might have isolated India and did not enhance its image in the outside world. Targets and goals were set, and India responded with creative dynamism, trying to meld traditional practices with modern challenges, although this was complicated by a rapid rise in population. The population was now over five hundred million. Maximum use was made of rivers to harness power, and India's industrialization and modernization progressed. Great Britain, Russia, and West Germany sponsored steel plants, while loans were taken from the United States. The specter of a burgeoning population was alarming, and so family planning was endorsed. Illiteracy continued to be rampant, with 70 percent of Indians unable to read or write, despite the excellent universities and colleges all over the country. Social change focusing on the caste system and passage of the Hindu Code Bill (regarding the position of women in India) were Nehru's main concerns. With Indian independence, women gained voting rights and the right to divorce. The minimum age for marriage was raised to eighteen for males and fifteen for females. The Hindu Succession Act of 1956 was another significant bill that protected the property rights of female children and gave them equal rights of inheritance.

In 1962 war broke out on the mountainous northeastern frontier with China. The Chinese overran the Indian positions, but fortunately they soon withdrew. This was humiliating for India and a terrible blow for Nehru who had worked hard to establish a good relationship with China. Nehru had advised the Dalai Lama to compromise with the Chinese when they overran Tibet. But the Dalai Lama and some of his followers chose to move to India, and his presence caused a certain awkwardness with China. However, in India the Dalai Lama, a Buddhist, was revered as an avatar and Buddhism was seen as an extension of Hinduism. The China incident of 1962 brought into focus a regular route from Tibet to Sinkiang, and the Kashmir settlement now began to take on new significance, with China hovering on the periphery of India.

Kashmir created a problem between Hindus and Muslims. The ruler was a Dogra Rajput Hindu, but most of his subjects were Muslim. Conflict between the two religions broke out when Muslim farmers rebelled against the feudal Dogra landowners. Fellow Muslims in neighboring Pakistan who wished to claim Kashmir supported this uprising. The Maharaja, who wished to belong to secular India rather than Pakistan, appealed for help. Nehru would not give up Kashmir to Pakistan. It was a very complicated, bitter dispute over Kashmir, encompassing canal waters, refugees, property, and assets. One of the motives for not giving up Kashmir was its role in India's defense against China, apart from Nehru's vision of a secular democracy in India.

Wars with Pakistan

On October 21, 1947, Sheik Abdullah, the Lion of Kashmir, the Muslim mystic who had often been jailed because he had demanded a Muslim share in the administration of the state, informed Delhi that Kashmiris wanted freedom. Hari Singh implored for help from India to defend Srinagar from thousands of Pathans (semi-nomadic tribes, who inhabit the border areas of northwest Pakistan) who started to congregate east over the Indus. Jinnah attempted to involve Pakistan's army in the fray but did not succeed. It was an unofficial war with thousands of Hindu refugees fleeing into India.

When Jinnah died in September 1948, Pakistan was unstable, and chaos reigned until the first Pakistani Prime Minister, Liaquat Ali Khan, reorganized the Muslim League. Liaquat was assassinated while trying to make a treaty with Nehru. This was followed by many army coups and military alliances with Washington. Leaders like Ayub Khan and Zulfikar Ali Bhutto tried to negotiate a diplomatic settlement over the coveted valley of Kashmir. Constant exchanges of fire were sparked as the Rann of Kutch, two hundred miles from the Indo–West Pakistan border, was patrolled by Pakistani soldiers. Patton tanks and artillery fire were being tested and used by Pakistan.

There were two thousand violations of the cease-fire, according to a report from the United Nations. Eventually, an uneasy cease-fire was proposed by Ayub Khan. But the second Indo–Pakistan war was inevitable, and it occurred in 1965. India raised nine hundred thousand troops, gained a martial victory, and almost took Lahore. A peace conference organized by Premier Alexei Kosygin of Russia resulted in India and Pakistan promising to seek peaceful means to solve the territorial rights issue and withdrawing their forces.

Nehru's death in 1964 left India bravely attempting to become a self-sufficient industrial power. His Five-year Plans had run into trouble, and India was disenchanted with Nehru's regime. The country had to face an embittered Pakistan, a hostile China, an indifferent Russia, and a disapproving Western world. Lal Bahadur Shastri, a Congress Party member, was elected in the wake of Nehru's death. He died suddenly in 1966, and Moraji Desai, a senior Congress Party politician, moved into place with right-wing politics. However, he was regarded with suspicion, and the Congress Party leaders felt that they would have more control if they elected into power the daughter of Nehru, Indira Gandhi (no relation to Mahatma Gandhi). Her father had never given her a position in the government, though she was closely associated with politics and was even elected president of the Congress Party in 1959. Congress thought they could manipulate Indira and chose her as India's first woman prime minister.

Indira Gandhi

Indira Gandhi (1917–1984) was a shy widow when she was appointed prime minister. The only child of Nehru, she became one of the world's first women prime ministers. After studying at the University of Bengal and at Oxford University, Indira had joined the National Congress in its struggle for India's independence. In fact, Jawarharlal Nehru had given Indira Gandhi a long and deliberate preparation in democracy. On her thirteenth birthday, her father (who was then imprisoned by the British) began to write her a series of letters, which were later published as *Glimpses of World History*. Starting with the Greeks, Nehru wrote fascinating accounts of ancient Chinese kingdoms, Buddhism, the Moghuls, the Industrial Revolution, the history of India, and the need for democracy.

Indira's term as prime minister was turbulent, with infighting and political upheavals. She abolished the privy purses of the Maharajas, nationalized major banks, and implemented socialist policies that appealed to the masses. She increased price and trade controls and used the slogan *garibi hatao* (abolish poverty). Elected for three terms, she proved to be more dominant in Indian politics than her father. Astute and effective with her trademark short hair and father's aristocratic nose, Indira ruled with extraordinary authority. But the Congress unity splintered. The opposition had already split into the D.M.K. (Dravida Munnetra Kazagham) Party in Madras, the Jan Sangh Party in Madhya and Uttar Pradesh, the Communist Party in Kerala, and the Swatantara Party in Gujarat. Indira was supported only by two-thirds of the Congress Party when she dismissed Morarji Desai from the Finance Ministry.

Indira played a major part in the Indo–Pakistan War of 1971. At its creation, Pakistan was divided into East and West Pakistan, and these states were in constant conflict. West Pakistan was made up of Punjabis, Sindhis, Pathans, Baluchis, and Muslim refugees from India. East Pakistan was more homogenous, with a Bengali-speaking population. In 1971 East Pakistan revolted because in spite of its greater population, political power resided with West Pakistan. A bloody conflict between the two regions resulted in an exodus of some ten million Pakistani refugees into India. With tremendous calm, Indira intelligently pursued a friendship with the powerful Soviet Union, while Pakistan was backed by the United States and China. She signed a twenty-year treaty of peace, friendship, and cooperation with the Soviets and waited for international opinion to make her move against Pakistan.

This civil war disrupted Pakistan after twenty-one years of independence. East Pakistan was underdeveloped and kept under martial control by the army. Sheik Mujibir Rahman (1920–1975), the Bengali leader of the popular Awami League, demanded autonomy, control over foreign exchange, and a central government. In March 1971, talks failed, East Pakistan unfurled flags of independence, and Bangladesh was born. Troops from Pakistan under Tikka Khan opened fire on students' dormitories and arrested Sheikh Mujibir Rahman, along with thousands of others. Ten million people fled to India from war-torn Bangladesh. Finally, Indian forces struck Pakistan while Pakistan attacked airfields in Kashmir. While no word came from the international community, Indira Gandhi sought to help the Bengali freedom fighters. In retaliation, Pakistan coordinated a massive air strike and attacked twelve Indian airfields. The next day, Indian forces struck Pakistan. War ensued. Six days later, Bangladesh was liberated, and Pakistan teetered on the brink of collapse. India withdrew in triumph. Though it was an undeclared war for Pakistan, it resulted in Kashmir still unresolved and no hope of recapturing Bangladesh. Mujib took over as prime minister, and Bangladesh became a secular state on December 6, 1971.

Indira Gandhi was criticized for becoming increasingly authoritative at home, and India became known as the "country of Indira." Problems intensified with demonstrations, strikes, and sit-ins over inflation, and try as she might, Indira Gandhi could not prevent new taxes, explain the corruption within her party, or squelch the opposing Janata Party (People's Party) that was determined to bring down her government. In June 1975 she declared a state of emergency, suspending all civil rights. All opposition leaders were arrested, and ten thousand people were imprisoned.

Her downfall would come from within the family. Her youngest son, Sanjay Gandhi, was fast emerging as a leading political figure. Although he did not hold any position in the Congress Party, he became an authoritative figure because of his close association with his mother. He became a media icon who was seen and heard everywhere. Under his direction, the government launched two controversial programs, believing that they would solve India's problems. The first was a birth control campaign, based on sterilizing any man with more than three children, and the second was a slum-clearance program. Both programs were unpopular as well as insensitive, and they destroyed the support of the masses. In 1977 Indira lifted the emergency rule and announced a general election. Indians voted against Indira and the Congress Party, having been filled with fear and suspicion. They voted for the Janata Party, which stood against her dictatorship. After thirty years of power, Congress was displaced. However, in 1980 the Janata Party dissolved due to bitter infighting and scandals. Once more, the disillusioned India turned to Indira and the Congress.

Indira returned to politics with an unpopular Sanjay Gandhi ensconcing himself as the heir apparent. In June 1980, Sanjay Gandhi was killed in a plane crash. Devastated, Indira turned to her other child, Rajiv, an airline pilot. A quiet, calm person who never aspired to be a politician, Rajiv Gandhi acquiesced to his mother's pressure and was elected to the National Assembly in 1981, winning Sanjay's seat in Amethi.

During her third term in the early 1980s, Indira Gandhi was confronted by several states demanding separation from the central government. Sikh militants under the aegis of the Akali Dal (Eternal Party), and the main Sikh Party in Punjab were getting increasingly bolder in their agitation for a separate state of Punjab called Khalistan (Land of the Pure).

Rajiv Gandhi and President Zail Singh sought to undermine the radical Akali Dal Party by sponsoring an unknown fundamentalist, Sant Jarnail Singh Bhindranwale. Instead of destabilizing the Akali Dal, however, Bhindranwale established his headquarters at the Golden Temple in Amritsar, the holiest shrine of the Sikhs, and from here, he launched a campaign against the government. In June 1984, Indira Gandhi launched "Operation Bluestar." Seventy thousand troops surrounded the temple, and a massacre ensued. Tanks and artillery battered down the historic temple. The Sikhs were devastated and saw it as an outrage to their religion. Although it was a military success, Operation Bluestar led to large-scale riots and a legacy of hate, distrust, and bitterness. Indira became a hated enemy of the Sikhs. Four months later, on October 31st, as she walked to work from her home, Indira Gandhi was assassinated with thirty bullets by two of her own Sikh bodyguards, in reprisal for sending Indian troops into the Golden Temple in Amritsar.

Rajiv Gandhi

In the wake of Indira Gandhi's death, hundreds of Sikhs were targeted and murdered by Hindus in pursuit of vengeance. Just when India seemed to be on the brink of collapse, Rajiv Gandhi (served 1984–1991) was sworn in as prime minister. He was forty years old with an Italian bride, Sonia. His youth and inexperience, as well as his mother's murder, won him sympathy, a crucial factor in the elections. He seemed to continue India's political family dynasty. He did endeavor to establish new policies: he encouraged modern technology and foreign investment, eased import restrictions, and set up many new industries. However, the rural sector remained untouched, while the middle class benefited from many jobs. Unfortunately, Bofors, a Swedish arms manufacturer, embroiled Rajiv in a scandal regarding the illegal payment of millions of dollars.

Meanwhile, India's importance to Sri Lanka, (Ceylon under the British), which gained independence from the British in 1948, has always been significant. Most of the twenty million inhabitants of Sri Lanka are descended from Indian migrants who arrived there two thousand years ago. The Tamil Hindu minority of five million settled around Jaffna. They came from Tamil Nadu, South India. The Tamils have long felt that the Sinhalese Buddhist majority treats them as second-class citizens. Ethnic conflict between the two groups escalated in the 1940s when Sinhala was appointed the official language. The Tamils organized themselves politically, and soon violent incidents exploded, with young Tamils calling for a separate Tamil nation, Elam. The most militant were the Liberation Tigers of Tamil Elam (LTTE), founded by V. Prabhakaran. It appeared that South India was supplying support for Sri Lankan Tamils.

In India, police were busy rooting out sympathizers and impeding the flow of arms and equipment under the orders of Rajiv Gandhi. Rajiv feared that other powers would come to the aid of the Sri Lankan government, upstaging India. In 1986 Rajiv Gandhi met with V. Prabhakaran and J. R. Jayawardene, president of the United National Party of Sri Lanka, seeking peace. But the talks ended in failure, and fighting resumed. President Jayawardane signed a treaty with Rajiv permitting a seventy-thousand-strong Indian peace-keeping force to enter Jaffna and disarm the Tigers. The Sinhalese looked on the Indians as an occupying force, and the Tamils felt Rajiv Gandhi had betrayed them. A year later, Rajiv Gandhi was assassinated by one of Prabhakaran's libera-tors, a young woman suicide bomber who, under the guise of a party well-wisher, placed a garland of flowers on the prime minister at a rally near Madras in South India and caused his death.

In search of a new prime minister, the Congress Party turned to Rajiv's wife, Sonia, a naturalized citizen, but she firmly turned down the offer. The Nehru dynasty had ruled the country for thirty-eight years. Seventy-year-old P. V. Narashimha Rao from Andhra Pradesh, South India, was elected for the interim phase. With the support and acumen of finance minister Manmohan Singh, in June 1991 Rao launched the eco-nomic globalization of India, opening up world market invest-ment and securing ten billion dollars of foreign capital to fuel the stagnant Indian economy. Products and corporations such as washing machines, popcorn, IBM, General Motors, Pepsico, Kentucky Fried Chicken, and McDonalds brought comfort and prosperity to the affluent Indians. The stock market skyrock-eted, and Bangalore in South India became the Silicon Valley of India. Import duties came tumbling down, and ministers who had studied at Harvard and Oxford Universities encouraged investors to go to India and reinvent not only their lives but also those of the Indian people.

Rao soon was charged with several accounts of corruption, however, despite his promises of free meals for schoolchildren and maternity pay for poor mothers. In the elections, A. B. Vajpayee from the BJP (Bharitya Janata Party) was sworn in on May 16, 1996. He was forced to resign in twelve days as he was shunned by South Indian and Muslim politicians. Dev Gowda was the next person to be sworn in as prime minister, but he stepped down within a year because of socialist opposition. A. B. Vajpayee returned to power in 1998 and continues to hold the office of prime minister at this writing.

~ 12 ~
India Today:
Continuity and Technology

Winston Churchill once dismissed India as a mere geographical expression; a place that was no more a nation than was the equator (*The Economist,* August 16, 1997). Today, India is a nuclear power. India has launched space satellites and is one of the world's most exciting emerging markets—a country of unrealized potential. Economic liberalization and privatization have brought sweeping, dramatic changes, stimulating foreign investment and fostering an open society supportive of free economic enterprise. Life expectancy has gone up from thirty years in 1930 to sixty at present. This has resulted in a demographic explosion from three hundred fifty million in 1947, the year of India's independence, to one billion today. After fifty-four years, Indian democracy has survived and is held sacred, despite governments being voted in and out. Roads have been built and grain reserves monitored, and the ability to locate problem areas has helped in ending starvation. India as a democratic country has not resorted to coercive methods of population control.

A free and articulate press, a staggering variety of glossy magazines, a middle class exceeding the population of the United States, and a burgeoning judiciary that can overrule the government have all coalesced to make India a powerhouse, opening up to the rest of the world. By the late 1990s, Indian immigrant computer software professionals, along with immigrants from China, led nearly one-third of all new technology firms started in California's Silicon Valley.

On the economic front, India's current population of roughly 1.02 billion thrives predominantly on agriculture. Nearly two thirds of the labor force are employed by agriculture, followed by the service sector at 18 percent and industry at 15 percent. However, the composition of the gross domestic product (GDP) is quite different. Nearly 51 percent of the GDP is generated in the service sector, whereas agriculture and industry contribute the other half roughly equally.[1] What one U.S. dollar could buy in the United States might require considerably less than a dollar's equivalent in Indian rupees to buy in India. From another angle, an individual earning a dollar per day in the United States would be considered very poor; a person earning Rs. 48 per day in India is not that poor and would probably belong to the lower middle class. Dividing Indian GDP by the prevailing nominal rupee–dollar exchange rate could be quite misleading.

India's agricultural production has grown steadily over the years to around two hundred million metric tons in recent times. Much wastage can be averted if India liberalizes free movement of grain across the country and offers its exports freely to developing nations. Right now there are restrictions and checkpoints, entailing payment of *octroi*—a municipal levy—and bribes. There are thus costs and hindrances to free movement of food grains from one part of India to another. So there are surpluses in some parts and shortages in others.

---

1. *CIA Fact Book on India 2001* and the Economic Survey of the Ministry of Finance, Government of India, 2001, 2002.

In the 1980s, the government began to realize that the centralized planned approach to growth adopted at independence had outlived its usefulness. Economists had recommended such an approach to allow India to quickly catch up with the developed world. Under the leadership of Jawarharlal Nehru, India had adopted a comprehensive policy regime of industrial licensing and directed growth. Public sector investment was central to this growth model, and the government invested in steel plants, nuclear plants, defense equipment production centers, power generation, and a host of other sectors. Private-sector entry was totally ruled out or restricted, and most other sectors were reserved for small-scale industries in the name of protecting the rural population that was so dear to the heart of Mahatma Gandhi.

This comprehensive and planned model of growth slowly bred distortions and inefficiencies. The reasoning behind this is understandable as the country had just emerged from more than two centuries of foreign occupation that had bled it of precious natural resources. Hence, exports were deemphasized. This meant, however, that the country was shielded from foreign competition and the infusion of new technology. This encouraged complacency and sloth, resulting in low productivity.

Further, the need for licensing to participate in any sector or to expand capacity meant that bureaucrats dictated what economic activity took place in the country. This gave rise to favoritism and corruption. The country realized this and slowly liberalized these rules. The escalation in oil prices due to the Gulf War in 1990 and the sudden drying up of foreign remittances from workers in the Gulf region saw India face a crisis in its balance of payments. For the last twenty years, the

Gulf had invited Indians to work in various regions. Indians earned good money, which was nontaxable, and thus the Indian workers were able to send money home to their families. This was one of the most important sources of foreign exchange. India went to the International Monetary Fund and came back with a loan and a bold plan to completely unshackle the economy. The sleeping tiger was awake and uncaged. Trade policies have dramatically reduced customs duties, accelerating significant growth in foreign investments.

This resulted in spectacular growth for the first two years in 1992–1993 and 1993–1994 after the initial stagnation in 1990–1991 and 1991–1992. For the first time, consumers had real choice in durable and nondurable consumer goods. Imports were liberalized, and people realized that this need not result in immediate re-colonization. There was a feeling of unease that a liberal import of foreign goods would mean dependence on foreigners. The experience of the East India Company coming into India and then ruling the country for two hundred years is a specter of re-colonization and is the undercurrent of Indian reluctance to embrace all things foreign.

One of the shining success stories of the liberalization era was the emergence of India as a global software powerhouse. About one hundred eighty-five of the Fortune 500 companies outsource their software requirements to Indian software houses. The software industry has enhanced India's image globally. In 1999, there were more than six hundred Indian-based software companies—employing over two hundred eighty thousand computer engineers.

One of the reasons that the software industry succeeded spectacularly was the near-complete absence of government controls on the sector. Thus, the telecommunication sector—a vital backbone to growth of information technology—is witnessing hectic activity today. India has many obstacles to overcome on its way to becoming a developed nation—a status that it enjoyed centuries ago before foreign exploitation. The fact that the governments at the center have featured multiparty coalitions has not helped, either. Decision-makers have to satisfy many constituents, compared to just one's own party members. Each member party in the coalition wants some special requests satisfied in return for their support. This may not result in rational economics. One may also have to accommodate coalition members as members of the Cabinet, leading to a larger size than is necessary. Simultaneously, this signals the rise of hitherto oppressed voices and a true federal structure of governance. One major challenge is how India can remain an integrated yet diverse nation. Overpopulation and unemployment is another problem, with 80 percent of Indians living in rural villages and the remainder residing in over two hundred towns and cities. Nearly one-third of the country lives below the poverty line.

Many provincial-level governing entities have moved ahead with their own measures to achieve dynamic growth and prosperity. This has been brought about by the decentralization of power, which has led to the emergence of self-reliant women in local administrations. Women form one-quarter of India's urban workforce. Many are activists or politicians. They also hold high-level management jobs, work on space programs, and head police departments, as well as following the traditional routes of becoming teachers and nurses.

India produces nearly one hundred twenty thousand engineering graduates annually—double the number produced in the United States. India also has a young population, compared to much of the developed world, and, hence, Indian skills should continue to be increasingly in demand globally. In the short term, India can look ahead to a period of faster growth. In the long term, its intellectual capital should enable it to achieve a higher growth rate, thus allowing the nation to realize its true potential. Japanese and American companies recently have entered joint venture agreements with Indian businesses.

Since 1947, India has been a working democracy in a multiethnic, multilingual, multireligious unified country. Although primary education was neglected in the years following independence, it is now being enforced after Indian leaders realized that universal literacy was the key to economic output. Urban India represents national politics, policies, planning, media, universities, armed forces, science, technology, and business. Rural India is the India where life continues in a traditional manner. The two must merge, with illiteracy reduced, poverty wiped out, education expanded, and health care promoted. Only then can India be strengthened.

Rapid advances in technology have brought in TV, computers, pagers, and cell phones, altering traditional lifestyles, along with fast-food culture. Five-star hotels, cars, refrigerators, washing machines, and dance clubs are available for those who can afford them. The debate over whether India should become "Coca-Colonized" by Western culture is still being discussed. Will alien influences disrupt Indian society? The jury is still out. Meanwhile, American TV shows, basketball, and veggie burgers are becoming very popular. Instead of the black and white state-run television channel, there is now a blitz of fifty vibrant satellite channels offering CNN, BBC, and B for U—a hybrid Indianized MTV program with glamorous and savvy veejays speaking a mixture of Hindi and English, a *masala* of sorts.

Many obstacles face contemporary India. Secessionist problems have been escalating in Kashmir. There have been numerous killings and much political turmoil, now more than at any other time since Independence. India's relationship with Pakistan reveals brokered peace negotiations over the territory of Kashmir, with both countries claiming to have nuclear capability. The internal divide between urban and rural India is another problem. Attitudes to sex, divorce, and marriage are rapidly changing in urban India. There are more marriages settled by the partners concerned rather than the parents and well-wishers. However, most marriages are still arranged by the parents who often consult astrologers. In general, the boys and girls are often relieved they do not have to seek partners for themselves or go on dates as it is done in the Western world. Alliances are often created for political and commercial reasons. The couples in urban areas do meet before the wedding and get to know each other, but this is not so in the villages. Matchmaking is mostly done through marriage bureaus, newspaper advertisements, and personal contacts. This kind of marriage is based on the linking of families and communities, not merely a man and woman being brought together in romance and matrimony.

The United States in particular has been a willing recipient of the India buzz over the past few years. *Vogue* magazine often incorporates color fashion features on India and Indian fabrics. Madonna appeared at the 2000 MTV Video Music Awards on stage surrounded by Odissi dancers, wearing mehndi (traditional body paint), and with a vermilion mark on her forehead. Bindis (the colored dot on the forehead) are the rage, and pop

143

Bride at wedding ceremony in South India (courtesy of Robert Arnett, India Unveiled*).*

singers don nose and toe rings. In the United States, the energetic Bhangra beat music from Punjab is now being played at proms and dances, while Ayurveda and yoga are becoming healthy solutions to a stress-filled lifestyle. Indian painters (M. F. Hussein, Anjolie Menon), writers (R. K. Narayan, Arundhati Roy, Romilla Thapar), musicians (Ravi Shankar, L. Subbramanian, L. Shankar, Hariprasad Chaurasia, Bismillah Khan), and dancers (Alarmel Valli, Briju Maharaj, Malavika Sarrukai, Dhananjayans) are respected internationally. Popular films (India produces one thousand a year in twenty languages) bring romance, music, color, drama, and escapism to the Indian filmgoer. Good and evil, action, much dancing, lots of music with at least seven songs, fights, comedy, and an intense love story are the main ingredients for blockbusters. A happy ending after a three-hour extravaganza is mandatory. There is hardly any kissing, and passion is sublimated in the mind of the filmgoer. The sumptuous, exotic cinema affectionately called Bollywood (Bo for Bombay and a nod to Hollywood) is the rage in Asia, Africa, and the Middle East and in any country where an Indian lives and works. Interestingly, no one wants to see a film on poverty or unemployment. However, social themes like dowry, evil landlords, villainous politicians, and oppression of women are all explored. Playback film singer Lata Mangeshkar made it into the *Guinness Book of Records* for singing the greatest number of songs in a lifetime: fifty thousand songs in a career spanning sixty-two years. Hindi (Bollywood) films like *Lagaan* and *Devadas* have been nominated for Oscars.

In South India, in 1967, the Congress Party was defeated and the DMK (Dravida Munnetra Kazagham) Party rose to power. The election was won through vigorous campaigning and through films written, directed, and performed by DMK members. Politics in South India have been dominated by film celebrities. M. G. Ramachandran, a swashbuckling hero in films, was elected chief minister, and M. Karunanidhi, a prolific writer of screenplays with vitriolic dialogue, also became chief minister. Today, a woman film star, Jayalalitha, who often acted with M. G. Ramachandran, is the chief minister.

On July 18, 2002, seventy-one-year-old bachelor, Dr. A. P. J. Abdul Kalam, born in a boatman's family in Rameeswaram in South India, became the newly elected president of India, winning the elections by an overwhelming majority and with the backing of India's ruling coalition and main opposition Congress Party. He is the architect of India's missile program, scientific advisor to the prime minister, and a Muslim.

For all its flaws and burdens of poverty, corruption, and illiteracy weighing against democracy, India is the ninth-largest industrial economy in the world. Nehru had stressed university teaching at the expense of village literacy. Today, because of his foresight, thousands of world-class Indian engineers are in demand and are valuable global contributors, while the common villager is out of step with the world today. This critical issue is being remedied, though at a slow pace. The challenge is to stand for openness and tolerance. However, Indians are proud of their unique democracy and still have a vision of their dreams being fulfilled. The cultural mosaic is not only astonishing but also extraordinary as India continues to grow as one nation. Four thousand years of cultural and philosophical development in India have left deep imprints on society, with every Indian being familiar with fascinating stories, legends, and history, and suffused with a deep spiritual consciousness of a great heritage and civilization.

Blessings from a temple elephant (courtesy of Robert Arnett, India Unveiled).

Women bathing in the sea near Puri (courtesy of Robert Arnett, India Unveiled).

PART II

LIVING TRADITIONS:
RELIGION AND CULTURE

Male pilgrims in Benares (courtesy of Robert Arnett, India Unveiled*).*

~ 13 ~
Religion

HINDUISM

Hinduism is practiced by 80 percent of India's population. The word *Hinduism* is derived from "Hindu," used mainly by invaders to identify the people who lived near the river Indus. Hinduism is a complex religion, abundant in mythology and practices.

Hinduism was not founded by one person but evolved from diverse beliefs founded in Vedic religion. The concept of cyclical nature is associated with the trinity of Gods: Brahma (Creator), Vishnu (Preserver), and Shiva (Destroyer). The major source of Hindu mythology is the Rig-Veda, a collection of more than a thousand hymns handed down orally for centuries before being written.

Hindus believe that everything that happens has taken place before and will happen again. They also believe there are all manner of truths and that one may reach the Supreme Power in many ways. The law of ethical cause and effect is called karma (actions carried out in one's current life will affect the circumstances of one's next life). A moral code or sacred obligation or duty is dharma. A disciplined life of dharma will affect one's karma, allowing one to be reborn into better lives during the repeated cycles of time. So dharma influences karma as well as reincarnation.

Hindu Gods and Goddesses

BRAHMA

According to myth, the Lord of the Universe was contemplating the cosmic egg as it lay on the surface of the ocean for a thousand years. A lotus sprang from his navel with the brilliance of a thousand suns, and from this emerged the self-created Brahma with the powers of the universe. The Creator Brahma has four faces that control all the directions and sides of the universe that he has created. Seated on a lotus, he holds the four Vedas (scriptures) in his hand. The cosmic lotus is the womb of the universe. Brahma is thus representative of wisdom, revelation, meditation, and knowledge.

VISHNU

As protector and preserver of the universe, Vishnu has various manifestations known as the Dashavatara (the ten forms of Vishnu). They are Matsya (a fish), Kurma (a tortoise), Varaha (a boar), Narasimha (a man's torso with a lion's head), Vamana (a dwarf), Parashuram (a sage with an axe), Rama (who killed the demon Ravana), Krishna (who killed evil Kamsa), and Buddha (founder of Buddhism). Kalki (a man riding a white horse) is the tenth avatar, who has yet to come into existence. It is believed by many that the order of the avatars represents the evolution of man from the fish to that of Parashuram, the mighty human. Lord Vishnu's wife is Lakshmi, the Goddess of good fortune and luck.

LAKSHMI

According to legend, Lakshmi sprang from the foamy waves of the ocean (churned by the Gods) with a lotus in her hand, radiating beauty. Another legend represents her as floating on the flower of a lotus at the creation. She is called "daughter of the sea of milk." There are no temples dedicated to her, but, because she is the Goddess of prosperity, she is worshipped by everyone. She represents material wealth and well-being. An ideal Hindu wife, she is auspicious and brings good fortune and fertility. Resplendently adorned, Lakshmi is always depicted seated on a lush blossoming lotus, the symbol of fertility. Two elephants on either side of her shower her with rainwater. According to myth, the ancient world was highly sophisticated and evolved, and it is believed that the first elephants were cousins of the clouds. They had wings and showered rain on the Earth. But cursed by a sage, these sky elephants lost this gift of flight and were thus confined to the ground.

SHIVA
Shiva is both benign and fearsome, creator and destroyer. Evoked by one hundred names, he is often worshipped in the form of the Lingam or the phallus, representing creative male energy, immovable. The Lingam is centered within the Yoni, the symbol of the female creative energy. This powerful image symbolizes opposing energies generating a creative union that sustains the universe.

KALI
Kali is imaged with a necklace of freshly cut heads, weapons, serpents, and blood. Regarded with both awe and fear, Kali expresses fury. This dangerous image reflects the disorder in life, the inexplicable accidents and horror that we must face in our world. Her horrifying image prepares the worshippers for

the trauma of everyday life. Paradoxically, she is also worshipped as a mother.

SARASWATI

The Goddess Saraswati is worshipped as an embodiment of the human intellect. She inspires culture, the arts, sciences, and poetry. Saraswati holds in her four hands a book for learning, the *veena* (stringed musical instrument) for the arts, sacred beads for meditation, and a water pot for the limitless stream of knowledge. She sits astride a swan or a lotus. In the north and south of India, Saraswati Festival is celebrated during spring. On this auspicious day, teachers, gurus, books, pens, instruments of learning, musical instruments, and even computers as tools of the trade are honored.

GANESHA

Ganesha, son of Shiva, is the remover of all obstacles. In Western India, large images of this elephant-faced God are installed and worshipped for seven days, during the Ganesha festival, after which they are immersed in the river or sea. This symbolizes our individual worries, trials, and obstacles being washed away by the rejuvenating waters.

In a myth relating to Ganesha's birth, it is said that Shiva was out hunting, and his consort Parvati desired to bathe without being disturbed. Using her powers, the sweat of her brow, and sandalwood paste, she created an image and breathed life into it. She made this boy child stand by her door and guard her while she bathed. Shiva returned home and was prevented from entering by the guard. Enraged, Shiva drew his sword and cut off the guard's head. Parvati was deeply distressed. Shiva promised to restore life to her creation. He sent his men to fetch the first animal head they found facing north. An elephant head was found and placed on the body of the guard. Shiva restored life to the guard to compensate for his hasty act. He promised Parvati that Ganesha, or the one with the elephant head, would be the beloved of all the people and worshipped by them before any other God. Lord Ganesha, also known as Lord Ganapati, uses a rat as a mount. The large elephant-headed deity rides a small mouse to demonstrate the control of indecisiveness and the easily distracted human mind. The mouse is the mind that scuttles this way and that; worship of Lord Ganesha provides steadfastness, control, and direction.

KRISHNA

Krishna is the eighth avatar or incarnation of Vishnu and perhaps is the most popular of all the deities. Legends and fables have grown around the Divine One since the time he appeared in the *Mahabharata* and delivered the celebrated song, *Bhagvad Gita.*

The story of Krishna is found in the Puranas where his early life is recorded with minute detail. His mischievous pranks as a child, the teasing of the *gopis* (maidens) by the river, and his exquisite flute music still give wondrous delight and inspiration to artists, musicians, singers, and dancers.

Hindu Festivals

Festivals in India are celebrated all the year round due to the diversity of its people, cultures, religions, and languages. Festivals are not only occasions for religious reverence but times for gaiety and feasting. They add color, pageantry, and a festive exuberance to the routine of everyday living. The family is strengthened and united by celebrations and rituals that mark important events. The community engages in devotion and excitement, and the "larger" family is brought together. Festivals honor Gods and deities, as well as celebrating the seasons, fertility, and birth. During festivals, rituals are performed to appease the dark forces and prevent their wrath.

Festivals also keep alive ancient artistic traditions. Families of craftsmen and artisans work throughout the year to provide the essential decorations and idols. Festivals are times of renewal. Walls are embellished with new designs, and thresholds are decorated with colorful rice powder and flowers. There is much feasting and exchanging of gifts. Chariots and other vehicles for the Gods are built and idols are sculpted. Since the majority of the citizens are Hindus, the Hindu festivals dominate the calendar. Dates for most of the festivals follow the lunar calendar.

PONGAL

Pongal (to overflow) is celebrated in January in Tamil Nadu, South India, when the Sun enters Makara (Capricorn). Makara is an aquatic animal of Indra, God of the heavens, who is supposed to control the clouds and cause seasonal rains. It is a celebration of the harvesting and a time for thanksgiving. A good deal of scrubbing, cleaning, painting and whitewashing takes place, and there are huge bonfires of old and unusable things in the house, thus symbolizing the driving out of evil spirits. The exterior of the home is decorated with intricate *kolams* (rice powder patterns). In the villages, huts are re-thatched. Families wear new clothes, and a mixture of freshly harvested rice is boiled in brand new pots to the point where it overflows.

Accompanied by the auspicious sound of conch shells and cries of "Pongal!" "Pongal!" the harvested rice is offered to the Gods. This ritual signifies abundance.

The following day, Mattu Pongal (Cattle Pongal) is celebrated in a boisterous fashion. The bull or cow is honored by the farmer for helping him in the fields and providing sustenance. Cows and oxen are bathed, fed, and decorated with garlands of flowers, turmeric, necklaces, and leaves. They are taken to the temple and paraded. The cattle are fed specially cooked rice, and they participate in a test of valor against young men in the *jallikatu*. The villagers turn out to watch the men pit their strength and courage against the bulls. In the days of old, jallikatu was a way for the daughters of local rulers to select a husband. The young man must mount the bull, cling to its neck or the hump on its back, and try to pluck the rupee notes attached between its sharpened horns. Cattle are essential to the livelihood of the rural population, and so they are celebrated and worshipped annually.

HOLI

During spring (March) in North India, when fields are golden with mustard flowers and wheat, Holi, the lively and boisterous festival of colors, is celebrated. Many people enjoy the festival by flying kites. People come out of their homes to throw a riot of colored powder and water at each other. There is revelry and song, and much boisterousness and exhilaration.

Various legends are connected with the festival's origin. One of them is the story of Prahalad, a boy child sent by the Gods to deliver the land of Braj from the cruelty of its king, Hiranyakashyap. In an effort to kill the child, the king's sister Holika, who was immune to fire, offered to take the child in

Caparisoned cow during Mattu Pongal festival.

her lap and sit in a fire that would consume him but not her. The boy's virtue left him untouched, however, and the wicked Holika perished. Holi gets its name from Holika, and every year images of Holika are burnt in bonfires

JAGANNATH CHARIOT FESTIVAL

Puri in Orissa has been an important center of Hindu pilgrimage as the abode of Lord Jagannath (a form of Krishna). Transcending barriers of caste and creed, he is worshipped by Buddhists, Jains, Shaivites, Sikhs, and even Muslims.

Every year in Puri, during June or July, three deities—Jagannath, his brother Balabhadra, and his sister Subadhra—are worshipped and placed on a car or chariot and carried in a procession through the streets.

In April, the deities are bathed in sandalwood-scented water and taken out on boats, while one hundred eight pitchers of water are poured over them. The deities are pronounced ill after this, and for fifteen days they remain in seclusion with apothecaries attending them. After this, the deities emerge from the inner sanctuary, rejuvenated and prepared for the journey of the Gods. It is said that their travel celebrates the journey of Krishna to Mathura.

To the rhythmic clang of gongs and cymbals, the deities are placed atop chariots, which are drawn with thick ropes by thousands of devotees with pomp and splendor in a mammoth procession. It is believed that whoever tugs the bedecked chariots will be delivered from the cycle of rebirths. By evening, the chariots arrive at the garden house and stay there for nine days, after which the return journey to the temple begins. The main car of the Jagannath rides on sixteen wheels, is fourteen meters high, and is hauled an inch at a time by four thousand temple attendants. This is the annual Ratha Yatra, which glorifies the divine values of love, compassion, and equality.

RAKSHA BANDAN

In North India during the month of August, brothers and sisters reaffirm their affection, faith, and trust in each other. The sister ties an amulet of colored thread or beads around the wrist of the brother. In turn, the brother gives her money while the sister feeds him with sweets. If the brothers and sisters are on different continents, the thread is sent in an envelope by mail. Nowadays the thread is decorated with semiprecious stones, or silver and gold threads, making it a thing of beauty. According to legend, it is believed that in a fierce battle between the Gods and demons, Lord Indra's wife, Indrani, having consulted scriptures, prepared an auspicious string to tie around Indra's wrist. Indra won the battle. The empowering aspect of the string (*rakhi*) has since then become a ritual bestowing good luck and blessings from woman to man.

Another such story is offered to us from the Rajput era. Rajput women tied this amulet on the wrists of their husbands and brothers as they went off to battle as protection against death and injury. This tradition was skillfully manipulated by Maharani Karmavati, queen of Mewar, who was under the threat of attack from an aggressor, Bahadur Shah. Brilliant and calculating, she instead sought out the Moghul King, Humayan, sent him a rakhi, and claimed him as her brother. This obligated him to protect her kingdom. The significance of the rakhi tradition has since then been adopted in homes to reflect bonds of kinship and affection between brother and sister.

NAVARATRI/DUSSERA

During the months of September and October, nine holy nights are observed. Houses are decorated with displays of dolls, toys, and images of Gods. In Mysore, elephant and horse processions are taken out daily. In Gujarat, the Dandiya (colored sticks) dance is performed by men and women with painted sticks. In the hills of Himachal Pradesh, deities are taken out of the temples in processions, musicians blow large horns, and colorful crowds accompany the deities.

The festival celebrates the victory of Lord Rama over the demon Ravana and his brothers Meghnath and Kumbhkaran. Ram Lila, a dramatic rendering of the life of Lord Rama, is performed on all ten days of the festival. On the last day, larger-than-life effigies of Ravana and his brothers, made of bamboo and paper and filled with firecrackers, explode in flames all over northern India, signifying the destruction of the forces of evil. Amateur actors perform all night and recreate the story of the *Ramayana* in every city and village. Large gatherings block off streets, and the play is performed to rapt audiences.

In West Bengal and many other parts of India, the festival celebrates the Goddess Durga's victory over the buffalo-headed demon Mahishasura. Durga, the eternal mother, is not only protective and mild but destructive as well, symbolizing feminine power and strength. Large *puja* altars with decorated images of the Goddess are raised, and on the tenth day they are immersed in the sea.

In South India, Dussera is celebrated as Navaratri (nine nights). On each night a different sweet dish is prepared and shared by family and friends. A special altar is made to Durga featuring dolls collected over the years by families. The street

Durga image immersed in Hooghly river, Calcutta (courtesy of Robert Arnett, India Unveiled).

and home are decorated with lamps, and all vehicles are adorned with marigolds, neem leaves, and bright flowers. The festival glorifies Shakti—the primordial female energy of the universe—as manifest in the Goddess Durga, who is the amalgam of Shiva, Vishnu, and Agni, and who killed the demons. This took her ten days, and the tenth day is celebrated as Vijaya Dashmi.

ONAM

The five-hundred-year-old spring festival of Onam celebrates the spirit of the popular King Mahabali in Kerala, in the form of sports and rituals during the months of August and September. According to legend, it is said that each year, when Onam is celebrated, the good king is invited into the homes of the people. It is believed that some Gods, envious of the king's popularity on Earth among his people, encouraged Lord Vishnu to intervene. Vishnu, disguised as a Brahmin dwarf (Vamana), visited the king and demanded from him three steps of land. Obliged to grant the wish of any passing sage, beggar, or Brahmin, the king granted his request. Vishnu revealed himself and grew stupendously tall, and with two steps he covered heaven and earth. Humbled by this great vision and revelation, the king asked Vishnu to place the third step on his head. The king's pride was thus humbled, and he was sent to the underworld but allowed to return annually.

The celebration of the king's yearly visit to Kerala includes a spectacular procession of magnificently adorned elephants. There are dance and music performances from the epics and folk tales, as well as exciting boat races. Elaborately decorated designs are created on the threshold of homes, with colored rice powder, flowers, and leaves.

Onam Festival, Kerala.

DIWALI

This festival is celebrated as Diwali in the north and Deepavali in the south, in the months of October and November. The festival of lights celebrates the return of Lord Rama, the hero of the epic *Ramayana,* to Ayodhya after a fourteen-year exile in the forest. Thousands of lights are placed on every available surface, houses are illuminated, and fireworks are set off to guide Lord Rama back to his home. There is much feasting, gifts are exchanged, new clothes are worn, and gold is bought. Business houses give a Diwali bonus to their employees, and residents renovate, paint, and decorate their homes. People also relish eating specially prepared Diwali sweets.

KARWA CHOUTH

In one story, Draupadi, wife of the Pandava princes in the epic *Mahabharata,* observed a fast for the safety of Arjuna when he went to war with the Kaurava's warriors. This belief continues today, as married women observe Karwa with day-long fasting and prayer to ensure marital happiness. Karwa Chouth is observed in the month of November by North Indians. Married women fast all day, drinking only fruit juice and water. The women listen to discourses in praise of the Goddess Parvati, who undertook great penance to marry the husband of her choice (Shiva). They then pray for prosperity and long lives for their husband and children, and they exchange gifts of clothing and sweets. When the moon is sighted in the sky, they seek its reflection in a vessel filled with water or through the mesh of the household sieve. After this auspicious sighting, they break fast and eat a special traditional meal.

KUMBH MELA

The Kumbh festival and fair is held in Haridwar (gateway to the abode of the Gods) in Uttar Pradesh every three years. According to mythology, the Gods and demons were at war with each other and churned the ocean for the nectar of immortality from the revered *kumbha,* or pitcher. A few drops of this divine nectar are believed to have fallen in four different locations, and since then saints and pilgrims visit and pay homage to these blessed sites.

KITE FESTIVAL

Kite flying is now a strong competitive sport in India, with traditional kite-flying days that fall on January 14 in Sankranti in the south and Basant, and on February 11 in Punjab. The basic kite is a square piece of paper with a streamer, and it may bear portraits of cricket players or film stars. Currency is attached to some kites, and bets are placed on the kites. The frame is made of split bamboo, and the string is often dipped in gum and powdered glass, making the thread a cutting edge to sever the kite strings of competitors. The taut, sharp string is attached to the kite. Then the kite flyer is ready for aerial duels using feinting, dipping, and twirling tactics. The sky becomes a mosaic of color due to all of the kites, some of which sport floral, birdlike, or geometrical designs.

ISLAM

Islam means submission to the will of God. Its followers constitute India's largest minority and are called Muslims. Muhammad, a merchant from Mecca in Saudi Arabia, founded the religion in 610 CE. He was regarded as a prophet or messenger of God. He received revelations from God (Allah) in the form of visions. These visions were codified and compiled in the Koran, the holy book of Islam, which contains laws that dictate how people may lead just lives. Islam recognizes only one God and preaches against idolatry: "There is but one God, Allah, and Muhammad is his prophet." The monotheistic religion preaches five tenets: One must (1) have faith in Allah, (2) pray five times a day facing Mecca, (3) make one pilgrimage to Mecca, (4) give alms, and (5) fast during the ninth lunar month, Ramadan. Sufism is a branch of Islamic philosophy and is based on religious tolerance, self-denial, and abstinence. Sufis believe that entering into a trancelike state during devotion brings one closer to Allah.

Id

Muslims in India celebrate the festival of Id at the end of the ninth month of the Muslim calendar. It commemorates Ibrahim's (Abraham's) trust in God as he prepared his only beloved son for sacrifice as demanded by God. Impressed by Ibrahim's faith and obedience, God finally asked him to sacrifice a lamb instead. On this day, every Muslim family sacrifices at least one lamb, and part of the meat is donated to the poor and then the rest is shared by the family. Special prayers are held at mosques all over the country.

Ramadan

Ramadan is the holy month of fasting, which lasts for thirty days. The dates correspond to lunar reckoning and not the

Gregorian calendar. Thus, Ramadan falls at a different time each year. The holy book, the Koran—which means, "to recite" in Arabic—was revealed during this time. Muslims believe the 114 chapters of the Koran came to Mohammed as revelations from God. Muslims host Iftar evenings when the daily fast is broken with fruits and sweets. Muslims fast so they can understand the suffering of the poor. Food is often donated to mosques to be distributed to the poor.

SIKHISM

Today there are some eighteen million Sikhs in India, mainly in Punjab, Haryana, and Delhi. There are two hundred Sikh Gurudwaras (places of worship) in India; the most sacred one is situated in Amritsar. In the fifteenth century, Hindus and Muslims lived together in an uneasy truce. Guru Nanak (1469–1539), a social and religious reformer, founded the Sikh ("to learn") faith to bridge the chasm between the two religions. He introduced new teachings with an emphasis on karma, good actions, universality, and brotherhood. Born at Talwandi in the Sheikhpura district of Pakistan, Guru Nanak always showed great interest in spiritual matters, spending much of his time in the company of ascetics and holy men. For thirty years he traveled all over India as an ascetic, preaching his religion of truth and equality. By combining the faiths of Hinduism and Islam, he provided a vision for brotherhood that was an astonishing ideology by today's standards. Guru Nanak believed in the "True One," a God with no form and no reference to either Hindu or Muslim conceptions. He rejected the caste system and its rituals. Yet he also believed in reincarnation and the

Sikh Pilgrim (courtesy of Robert Arnett, India Unveiled).

repetitive cycle of birth, influenced by karma. He reached out to the common man and emphasized that if one's actions are not good, then one's sins cannot be washed away by all the waters of the Ganges.

When Babur invaded India, he took Guru Nanak prisoner. When he learned that Nanak was a saintly guru, he decided to free him. However, Guru Nanak refused to be freed unless all prisoners were freed. With reluctance, Babur was forced to set all the prisoners free.

Sikhism became infused with ideas of freedom and nationalism. Large numbers of people were converted to the new faith. Soon Guru Nanak came to be revered as a prophet freeing people from the bondage of superstition and the tyranny of fundamentalism. He died at the age of seventy in 1539. This Sikh faith made rapid progress under his successors. There were nine other Sikh gurus (thought to be reincarnations of the Guru Nanak) who guided the religion and its followers. The *Adi Granth,* containing the teachings and hymns of the gurus, became the Bible of the Sikhs. Some gurus were persecuted by Moghul rulers, tortured and martyred. Others like Guru Har Govind (1606–1644) were not only spiritual leaders but also military leaders who organized armies. Still others were imprisoned or beheaded, but the gurus continued to propagate the faith.

Guru Gobind Singh (1666–1708) was the last guru. It was he who instituted the Khalsa brotherhood in an attempt to give a practical, outward, symbolic manifestation of the Sikh faith. His male followers began to add Singh (Lion) after their names. They wore five symbols or articles of faith on their persons at all times: *kara* (steel bracelet), *kachcha* (undershorts), *kirpan* (sword of honor), *kesh* (long hair covered by a turban), and *kangha* (comb). These symbols would embody a powerful notion of communal identity. In the seventeenth century under Guru Gobind Singh, the Sikh religious movement changed from a pacifist movement to a militant brotherhood due to persecution at that time. Most Sikhs joined the army. In the early 1980s a certain section of Sikh extremists in Punjab aspired for separatism in the form of Khalistan. The political situation has yet to be resolved.

The birth anniversaries of Guru Nanak and Guru Gobind Singh are celebrated with religious fervor and devotion by Sikhs. Processions held at the Gurudwaras are illumined, and food and sweet offerings are distributed to the worshippers. The Golden Temple of the Sikhs sits resplendent in Amritsar amid a serene expanse of water and space. The temple itself is a small square two stories high with a dome. Gold leaf was applied in the nineteenth century after the temple had been destroyed and rebuilt many times. The Sikhs had endured the most terrible persecution at the hands of the Moghul emperors in the seventeenth and eighteenth centuries.

JUDAISM AND CHRISTIANITY

Small communities of Jews settled in Malabar, Kerala. The earliest reference to their existence is a tenth-century charter by which the Chera king, Ravi Varman, gave land and privileges to a Jew named Joseph Raban. Another tradition tells of a large settlement in Cochin, in the first century CE. A very small Jewish community has existed in Cochin for well over a millennium. The Jews of Cochin pride themselves on an ancestry that goes back to the sixth century BCE. At this writing, there are only twenty-eight Cochin Jews remaining. Emigration to Israel has reduced their numbers.

Christianity took root in 52 CE with the arrival of St. Thomas, one of the disciples of Christ. An old tradition tells us that the Indian king Gondophernes asked for a skillful Syrian architect to build him a new city. The envoy returned with St. Thomas who spoke to the king of a heavenly city not made by hands and converted him and many members of his court to Christianity. St. Thomas died a martyr's death, and Roman Catholics in India believe that the tomb of St. Thomas is to be found in the San Thome Cathedral, Mylapore, Chennai, in South India.

In the sixteenth century and afterward, the Catholic and Protestant missionaries from the Dutch, Portuguese, and English settlements converted the Indians to Christianity. Christianity has been long-lasting mainly in Goa and Kerala. Hindus were baptized and converted for many reasons: some gained education at mission schools and were helped by mission hospitals, others were benefited by food, and several were freed from the caste system. Missionaries were responsible for compiling the first bilingual dictionaries and grammars.

On December 25th all over India, carols are sung, and people attend parties and dances. Midnight services are held in churches. Busy bazaars sell Christmas trees, baubles, and trinkets. There is much gift exchanging and sending of Christmas cards, many with Indian traditional motifs and designs, with Mary draped in a sari holding a dark-skinned baby Jesus.

BUDDHISM

Today, less than 1 percent of India's population is Buddhist. However, Buddhism has more followers in Southeast Asia.

Established around 500 BCE, Buddhism urges the individual to follow the eightfold path: to believe right, speak right, desire right, think right, behave right, do right, live right, and meditate. Buddhism emphasizes nonviolence. Buddhists are vegetarians.

There are two main doctrines in Buddhism, Mahayana and Hinayana. Mahayana Buddhists believe that the right path of a follower will lead to the redemption of all beings, and Hinayana believe that each person is responsible for his or her own fate.

ZOROASTRIANISM

One of the oldest religions, Zoroastrianism was founded in Persia by the prophet Zoroaster in the sixth or seventh century BCE. Zoroaster was born in Mazar I Sharif in Afghanistan. His teachings spread all over Iran, to Karachi in Pakistan, and to Mumbai in India. The followers of Zoroastrianism, known as Parsis, fled to India to escape persecution in Persia. According to legend, boatloads of Parsis fleeing from Persia waited off the coastland of Gujarat for permission to land. The Hindu king of that time did not want an alien religion in his land. He sent a glass of milk to say that India was already saturated with people and had no place for more. The Parsis added sugar to the glass, saying that they would be like the sugar in the glass, enhancing the Indian culture without changing its appearance. They promised not to intermarry and not to promote their religion.

Zoroastrianism formulates the belief that God is omnipotent and invisible. Good actions and good words are the essence of a peaceful life. The Zend-Avesta scripture of the

Parsis constantly elaborates and analyzes the forces of good and evil. Ahura Mazda is the God of Light symbolized by fire. Parsis worship in temples where flames burn eternally as a symbol of their God. To preserve the purity of the elements, they neither cremate nor bury the dead; instead, the bodies are left in the Towers of Silence where they are devoured by vultures.

There are around eighty-five thousand Parsis in India today. Parsis celebrate Navroz, which is their New Year, *Nav* meaning new and *Roz* meaning day. On this day, Parsis prepare lavish feasts, exchange gifts, and give alms to the poor. After this, each family visits the fire temple.

JAINISM

Jainism emerged around the sixth century and is closely linked to Buddhism. Founded by Mahavira, its rigid tenets instruct followers of Jainism to be vegetarians and to avoid causing injury to any living creature. Apart from meat and fish, Jains also abstain from eating onions, potatoes, garlic, and other vegetables that grow underground. They do not eat after dark to avoid accidentally consuming any insects. There are seven million Jains living mainly in Mumbai (Bombay), Gujarat, Punjab, and Delhi.

Following are the major Jain festivals:

MAHAVIR JAYANTI
The birthday of the last Tirthankar (prophet) is celebrated throughout India and especially in Bihar, the birthplace of Mahavira in April and May. The festival includes a grand

Procession of Jain devotees (courtesy of Robert Arnett, India Unveiled).

chariot procession, community worship, discussions, discourses, and seminars.

PARYUSHAN MAHAPARVA

Another important festival for the Jain community in India is observed for eight days in August–September, from the twelfth day of the fortnight of the waning moon until the fourth day of the waxing moon. This is the time for reflection on good and bad actions committed over the past year. Jains fast and take vows during this time. The monks read the scriptures, and followers initiate a disciplined meditation to seek forgiveness, charity, simplicity, honesty, detachment, and humility. It is also the time of monsoon weather, and by meditating in one place monks do not run the risk of accidentally causing death to any insect or small creature that has emerged during this season.

Gopuram in Hampi mid 15th century (courtesy of Robert Arnett, India Unveiled*).*

~ 14 ~
Customs and Rituals

BINDI

The colored mark or dot on the forehead, the *bindi*, worn by both men and women in India is endowed with multiple meanings. In meditation, the spot between the brows is a vital area of concentration and focus. It is also the center of spiritual energy within the human body, opening like a third eye to enlighten. In yoga, the activation of this third eye overcomes ego. The mark is considered a sign of *sowbhagya*, or good fortune, for married women. Some women believe that the larger the dot, the longer the life of the husband. In one of their marriage rites, the Santhals, a tribe in Bihar, represent the idea of eternal union between husband and wife. At the ceremony, a few drops of blood are drawn from the couple and mixed; the husband applies this to the forehead of the wife, and what remains is added to milk and water for the couple to drink.

The bindi is available now in every color imaginable, as well as gold, silver, jeweled, with a variety of designs, and in powder, liquid, or cream form. There are even stick-on bindis in assorted shapes.

THE SACRED COW

The cow is central to Hindu life. It has symbolized Mother Earth ever since the Vedic Age, when people depended on the cow for milk, byproducts, status, and trade. The Aryans invoked the fire God Agni by ritually burning sacred wood on an altar. This fire was kept alive by pouring melted butter, while milk was offered to the Gods. Later, in the period depicted in the the *Mahabharata,* ghee or clarified butter from the cow was essential to rituals. Lord Krishna, the cowherd, also gave importance to the cow. He was called the protector of cows.

Even today, the usefulness of the cow is significant, demanding respect and gratitude. Homeless cows are allowed to wander in the streets unharmed, and many are adopted by temples. The cow is the surrogate mother who provides the essential life-giving force, milk. Even the dung of the cow is used as fertilizer and fuel. In the villages it is used to coat the walls and floor of huts, ridding the ground of bacteria.

Nandi, the bull associated with Lord Shiva, sits in a prestigious position before him at the altar. Devotees whisper wishes into its ear, and it is said that these are conveyed to Lord Shiva, who grants them.

MEHNDI (HENNA)

In north India, once a girl's marriage date has been arranged, an auspicious day is chosen to apply *mehndi* on her hands, arms, and feet as a good omen. The ritual is accompanied with songs to the beat of the drum. Professional mehndi designers are in great demand. Patterns assume the form of geometrical

Blessings taken from the sacred cow.

Nandi bull.

and floral designs, as well as patterns based on the sun and moon. Often the name of the groom is written within the pattern. It is said that he will spend many intriguing moments tracking the letters of his name on the arms and feet of his new wife.

The leaves of the behendi shrub are ground with turmeric and some herbs to form a fine powder, which is then sifted through a fine cloth and let sit for an hour to form a paste. Lemon juice and sediment from strained tea or coffee are added to create a deeper and lasting hue. Today plastic cones have taken the place of nimble fingers, and the use of henna to decorate the feet or hands is in fashion in Western countries.

RANGOLI AND KOLAMS

Each morning, soon after the sun has risen, the threshold area of the home is swept clean and is sprinkled with water. The woman of the house, with bare fingers, traces elaborate, decorative designs from white or colored powder to usher Gods and Goddesses and good fortune into the home. Petals of flowers are also used and interspersed with leaves. Most of the designs are buds or blossoms of flowers, as well as leaves. Other popular designs include the shape of the mango fruit; animals like the cow, bull, elephant, eagle, or horse; and geometrical designs. During festivals they become elaborate, replete with images of chariots, temples, and of deities.

Each morning, the previous day's design is swept away to usher in a new one, symbolizing the ephemeral quality of life. The artists do not sign their names to their artistic work. The art is transferred from generation to generation in families. Magazines publish new designs every month.

Mehndi decorating artist Bharti Ashani.

Malathi Iyengar, Rangoli artist.

The Sari

The sari is mentioned in Hindu literature and depicted in Hindu painting as far back as 3000 BCE. Historically, the material and drape of the sari provide evidence of the wearer's marital status, religion, occupation, or origin. The term *sari* is derived from the Sanskrit word *cheera*, which means a length of cloth. It is believed that the needle was considered a weapon, and so the sari cloth was never stitched. With the arrival of the British, significant changes in the Indian sari occurred. The British disapproved of diaphanous and sheer saris as they considered them too titillating. So before a sari was draped around the body, a blouse and petticoat or underskirt was used, and this found favor in the eyes of the British and the missionaries.

A sari can be quite useful. The edge of the sari that is draped freely over the left shoulder can be tied into a knot to hold loose change or a bunch of house keys. The sari can be draped over the head to protect one from the sun or rain, and to wipe the sweat off one's brow. Old saris are cut up and sewn into pillowcases or quilts, exchanged for stainless pots and pans, redyed, or used as rags. Borders are removed and attached to children's skirts.

Pleats are all-important and may be tucked in at the waist. Legend has it that Vayu, the wind God, can whisk away any evil influence that might strike the woman in two important regions, the stomach and the reproductive organs, if she did not have the pleats for protection

Designs on the sari may illustrate the sun, moon, parrots, lions, mangoes, peacocks, lines and squares, flowers, buds, a layer of silver on gold, or vines. All are woven with meticulous detail.

Each state in India has its characteristic sari. Contrasting colors include red and saffron, as well as blue with purple; textures range from crisp organza to soft cotton, rustling silk, and thick brocade. They may be embellished with silver thread, dazzling sequins, or embroidered patterns. Auspicious reds are worn by the bride to evoke passion and good fortune, yellows and greens symbolize fertility for new mothers, white is ascetic and worn by widows because life without a husband is considered colorless, and blue is associated with yearning and longing for a beloved.

Sari worn in traditional manner.

SACRED TREES

Rama in the epic *Ramayana* was exiled into the forest from the city of Ayodhya. The female demon Tataka had used her evil power to make the land arid and desolate. When Rama arrived, she was vanquished, and the forest came alive with buds and blossoms.

Worship of trees in India is a veneration of fertility, growth, and the mysteries of organic nature. The tree symbolizes knowledge and spirituality. In ancient times, deities were worshipped in the open air under trees. Later, temples were constructed, but the tree remained an integral part of worship.

Trees are believed to be peopled with spirits, deities, and demons. According to the texts, conservation of the environment became a deliberate mission, and trees became objects of devotion, appeasement, and invocation. An early Buddhist legend tells us that Buddha was born as his mother Maya Devi held a branch of the flowering sal tree, and later Buddha received enlightenment while meditating under a bodhi tree (pipal tree). Sages taught their disciples in forests. Education was conducted in these verdant surroundings far away form the hustle and bustle of everyday life.

A verse in the poet Kalidasa's *Malavikagnimitra* lists ten trees and their longings. While waiting to burst into bloom, each tree demands a different response from a young and beautiful woman. The priyangu beckons for a touch, the bakula yearns for wine, the kurabaka desires caresses, the mandara awaits for gentle speech, the champa hopes for a sweet smile, the nameru aspires for song, and the karnikara demands dance.

~ 15 ~
Crafts

The Indian Arts Council defines India as an exhibition that never closes. Men and women work by the roadside, in narrow shop fronts, in backyards, in the precincts of temples, and in narrow alleys to fashion beautiful ritual, and household objects from the humblest materials. Whether it is a sculptor from South India, a weaver from Gujarat, a wood carver from the north, or a potter making a votive figure or a pot for cooking, each artisan is involved in continuing a five-thousand-year-old tradition.

LEATHER

Embroidered shoes are popular in southern Rajasthan. The *chappal* (sandal) appears in a multitude of versions ranging from a simple design to slippers with brass and silver thread. Today, there are many variations with chappals made from plastic or even old tires. Leather puppets are produced on the Karnataka coast, as well as in Andhra Pradesh. Jaisalmer is famous for camel-hide bottles with extravagant carved wooden stoppers.

PAPER

The palmyra leaf was used for writing and painting for many centuries. Emperor Babur is said to have introduced paper in the 1520s near Rajasthan. Sanganer is now the papermaking center in Rajasthan. Paper is made from cotton waste. Flower petals are introduced into the pulp, or the pulp is dyed to produce a marbled effect. Lime is often added to whiten paper. Papier-mâché is also a flourishing craft in Kashmir and West Bengal, where paper masks are worn in Kerala by Kathakali dancers.

POTTERY

There is a legend that explains how pottery, the oldest and simplest of handicrafts, came into being. The Gods and demons churned the primal ocean in order to extract nectar. Having obtained the nectar, they needed a vessel in which to contain it. So the God Vishwakarma molded a pot. The pot in India may be made from clay, terracotta, brass, copper, silver, or gold, and it always has had religious significance. It is auspicious and necessary for every religious ceremony, and if no image of a God is available for worship, a pot of water makes a substitute.

The potter's kiln is made of simple broken pots, and fuel may vary from straw or rice husks to wood, sawdust, and cow dung. In Uttar Pradesh, black pottery known as *bidri* is made exquisite with elaborate designs that are incised on its surface and filled with a silver paint made from a mixture of mercury and zinc.

During the festival of Ganesha, thousands of clay images of the God are made by the potter caste. These clay images of the elephant-headed God are later immersed in the sea or a river at the end of the festivities.

Clay images from Lord Ganesha festival.

Tens of thousands of images of the Goddess Durga, Shiva, her consort, and their four children are made for the Bengali festival of Durga Puja. The figure of the ten-headed Goddess Durga may be thirty feet high and painted over with zinc oxide. The images are dried in the sun and then carried in procession and placed in the river. Durga images are also made of wood shavings, shells, glass shards, and even plastic bottles.

During Dussera celebrations, the evil king Ravana also appears in procession. The oversized clay effigies of Ravana are garlanded with fireworks, which are then lit and exploded. During Deepavali, the festival of lights, millions of clay lamps illuminate and decorate homes and temples throughout India.

Many Indian foods are cooked in clay pots. This imparts an earthen flavor that mingles with the herbs and spices, enhancing the taste. In Tamil Nadu on the day before Pongal, the harvest festival, all the old clay pots are smashed, and the kitchen is stocked with new ones. But clay pots are giving way to plastic pots these days. Clay storage jars in Gujarat are used for storing rice and grains, while potters have also been known to construct cupboards of unbaked clay to be used as cool refrigerators. The Gujarati women then whitewash and decorate the clay cupboards with tiny mirrors and relief and intricate motifs.

Jaipur pottery is remarkable for its mixture of ingredients. It contains no clay at all, only quartz, green glass, fuller's earth, borax, and gum. This is kneaded, flattened, and pressed into a mold. Then the pot is painted with outlines drawn in cobalt oxide and metal oxides. The bright colors appear after firing, when the oxide of the cobalt creates the characteristic startling blue of Jaipur pottery.

Hawa Mahal, Palace of the Winds, Jaipur (courtesy of Robert Arnett, India Unveiled).

Beautifully finished clay toys are made in Bengal and Lucknow, often in the shapes of people or animals. Terracotta horses stand guard outside most villages in Kudurai, Tamil Nadu. These horses are made in Salem or Pudukottai. They also are made in Bengal and in Bankura, Dharbanga, Bihar, and Gorakhpur, Uttar Pradesh. They are richly caparisoned with necklaces and even jewels and used as family deities. In rural areas, clay deities include images of the cobra, which is believed to intercede for the worshipper.

WOOD

India is known for its decorative woodwork. Skills are often passed down from father to son. In Punjab, North India, you can marvel at exquisitely wrought wooden balconies. Intricately carved brackets support floors in Gujarat houses, while the beams and shutters of Rajasthan reveal the mastery of the woodworkers. Wealthy homes in Madurai, Tamil Nadu, boast doors sixteen feet high and relief panels depicting hundreds of deities. The luxurious forests of Kerala provide wood suitable for carved panels, rosewood furniture, chests, and boxes studded with brass and ivory. Gujarat is the home of craftsmen who fashion bridal chests on wooden wheels (*patara*) that are strengthened with brass and iron. Today the boxes are made of sheet metal and painted over with pictures. In Kerala, craftsmen continue to make the nine-sided bridal chest made of jackfruit wood which holds the bride's jewels and spices.

In southern India, temples keep processional chariots can measure up to fifty feet in height and are carved with deities

Pottery horses stand guard outside a South Indian village.

and mythical animals. Scented sandalwood is used for carvings of deities. The Jagannath Temple in Puri, Orissa is one such temple. Chariots are still made in Andhra Pradesh, Tamil Nadu, Karnataka, Kerala, and Orissa.

DECORATIVE INLAY

Ivory inlay came into vogue during the Moghul reign, so while wooden articles were made by Hindus, the Muslims did the inlaying. All over the north of India, metalworkers practice their art on copper and brass, producing vessels with intricately traced designs. It was Shah Jehan who introduced the Italian craft of *pietra dura*, the inlaying of precious stones into marble. The descendants of the artisans of the Taj Mahal still continue the tradition of using forty-two varieties of stone in a single motif.

PAINTINGS

Wall paintings by the women of Mithila in Bihar adorn the walls of their homes and illustrate their lives. The bold and dramatic fabric paintings of Bengal contain mythological themes, while in Orissa, themes from the Vedas are painted on a cloth base, treated with earth and tints from stone, and coated with lacquer. Rajasthan is the place for earth colors. There, a range of designs in black, red, orange, and olive green can be seen on fabrics and patterns on women's skirts. Cloth is painted on scrolls that look like gigantic picture books, which are carried around by the Bhopas who sing of folk heroes and use the scrolls for visual demonstrations.

STONE CARVINGS

Stonecarvers in Jaipur learn their techniques from their gurus and manuals (*shilpa shastra*) in accordance with ancient aesthetic codes. From sandstone in Mirzapur, Uttar Pradesh, carvers in settlements fashion Hanuman, the six-foot-high monkey God. Soapstone, found in a number of places in India, is used for decorative inlaid boxes, bowls, small ashtrays, and vases.

Stones used for temple carvings are selected on auspicious dates, and sometimes sculptors (*sthapathi*) will observe a fast for a day and pray to Lord Ganesha, before starting their work.

In South India, a region of diverse and rich sculptural traditions, stone sculpture is taught in Mamallapuram, a town with thousands of stone monuments. Made of black granite extracted from quarries nearby, the deities extend twenty feet in height, following the classical Chola styles. The Meenakshi temple in Madurai displays a profusion of sculpture with the thousand-pillared mandapas, pillars of stone, and larger-than-life-sized reliefs. The size of the waist and torso, the length of the nose and eyebrows, and the distance between the eyes are specified with precise measurements in the ancient manuals. The sculptor expresses his own identity and style within this formal framework.

The sensual and erotic temple sculptures of Khajuraho, in Madhya Pradesh, were created by the Chandella Dynasty, who are believed to be descendants of the moon. Hemawati, a young widowed daughter of a Brahmin priest, was believed to have been seduced by the moon God while she bathed. When the moon God prepared to leave, the young woman threatened to curse him, and so the moon God promised her the birth of an all-powerful son. The child was Chandravarman, founder of the Chandella Dynasty. Chandravarman is said to have had a dream in which his mother told him to build temples that revealed human passions and the futility of desire.

For the next one hundred years, eighty-five temples were constructed, and the city of Khajuraho was named for the Khajur or date palms that dotted the countryside in profusion. As there was no mortar in those days, each stone was cut to fit. Every inch of stone is covered with three-dimensional sculptures of beasts, courtesans, nymphs, bejeweled Gods, Goddesses, demons, parades, royal ornamentation, feasting, dancing, and mortals in the throes of fear, jealousy, revenge, lust, passion, and romance. The limbs are smooth, free from hair, ageless, and supple. The poses and gestures express fecundity, vegetative abundance, fruit-laden surging sensuality, and a rhythmic vitality. Everywhere there are carvings of amorous embraces and intriguing erotica. One discovers a striking, voluptuous woman removing a thorn from her foot, graceful dancing girls, and beauteous maidens writing letters, fondling babies, or playing music. Some say that these sculptures reminded the devotee to leave behind all thoughts of the mortal world when he entered the temple. Others believe that the temple was built during the period of a fertility cult, while still others explain that the integration of spirituality and eroticism symbolized the union of devotee with the divine.

Today only twenty-two of the eighty-five temples remain, and many have fallen into the hands of the invaders. The few

Heavenly nymph removing thorn from foot, Khajuraho temple, Chandella dynasty (courtesy of Robert Arnett, India Unveiled).

that remain owe their survival to the remoteness and inaccessibility of their location.

JEWELS

Certain gems are associated with different planets. When a Hindu buys jewelry, an astrologer is consulted before the purchase. The gem is evaluated to ensure that it coincides with the planet sign of the wearer, guaranteeing a positive and heavenly radiation beneficial to the body. So if your planet is weak, you may have to wear a coral set in a gold or silver ring. If you desire a blue sapphire, the jeweler will sell it to you and ask you to wear it for twenty-four to seventy-two hours. If there are no ill effects, you can keep the sapphire. Indians set great store on the astrological importance of gems and jewelry. Many look for the right stone to set in a ring before starting a new venture, be it a *chai* (tea) shop or a high-tech corporation.

Jewels not only adorn and beautify but also offer symbolic protection against evil forces. Colored precious and semi-precious stones have special meanings. Yellow (gold) reflects the rich harvest grain and is the color of Lord Vishnu, the protector of the universe, as well as the Goddess Lakshmi, the bestower of health, wealth, and prosperity. Red (rubies) is symbolic of love and belongs to the creator of the universe, Lord Brahma. White (diamonds) represents purity, knowledge, and truth and is the color of Lord Shiva. The parrot is the vehicle of Kamadeva, the God of love and passion, while the lotus symbolizes the universe and the sun as it spreads its large petals at dawn. Irrespective of religion, caste, or wealth, men, women and children have worn jewels not just for ceremonial

Head ornaments.

occasions but as part of their everyday lives. Jewelry could always be sold in times of pestilence, famine, or war.

South India offers an extravagant selection of jewelry. You can select jewels fashioned in diverse shapes, depicting a lotus, peacock, swan, parrot, snake, bird, or an intricate floral design. Gold ornaments set with precious stones are worn on the forehead. Many women wear waistbands of gold to accentuate the curve of the waist, and earlobes are pierced almost as soon as a baby is born. A typical ear ornament might consist of an ear stud of rubies and diamonds called the *kammal*. Below this hangs the *jhumki*, a bell-shaped eardrop in gold or studded with precious stones. The earring could be attached to the hair by another gold chain looped over the ear. Rural Tamil women also wear Paambadam, a solid mass of gold so heavy it stretches the earlobes down to alarming lengths. Most women also wear ankle bells in silver or gold with complex patterns.

North Indian jewelry is influenced by thousands of precious stones acquired by the Moghul Empire during the sixteenth and seventeenth centuries. Jewelry-making was at its height during this time. Fine pieces of workmanship, including necklaces, armlets, rings, and pendants, were designed in the Moghul period. Even weaponry often was made from precious materials. Many paintings reveal jugs, platters, cups, and bowls encrusted with pearls, emeralds, rubies, and diamonds. The Moghuls also loved bejeweled back-scratchers and fly-whisk handles.

In Kashmir, parts of West Bengal, and Orissa, filigree silver is a specialty, while enameling is prevalent in Himachal Pradesh. There is an abundance of silver in western India where there was much trade in silver with the Middle East and

Africa. Hyderabad is the central marketplace for dealing in cultured pearls.

Silver jewelry is more prevalent for ornaments of the feet. Anklets are joined with toe rings with a multitude of chains and embellished with silver sun- and moon-shaped discs. Toe rings are associated with marriage.

Despite advances in technology and equipment, the handmade jewelry of India continues to awe and inspire. Jewelers work with their hands and without the aid of machinery. The implements are few and simple: a furnace, a blowpipe, a small anvil, tongs, a hammer, pincers, a crucible, files, and chisels.

Necklace with pendant.

~ 16 ~
Music and Dance

MUSIC

Classical Indian music is identified as Hindustani in the north and Carnatic in the south. Music in India began with the chant, the recitation of Vedic hymns, rich in lyricism and philosophy. Later, melodies shaped the words, and the scale was expanded with flats and sharps and aesthetically flavored variations. Music has always had its roots in ritual. Along with dance it is one of the acts of worship in the form of religious hymns, songs, prayers, chanting and devotional rituals that have provided faith, joy, and solace for centuries.

Music has always been an integral part of Indian life, whether rural, urban, secular, or religious. Classical and folk melodies mark every aspect of life: birth, marriage, sowing, harvesting, and religious celebrations. Some of the popular instruments include the sitar, *sarod*, *veena*, *tabla*, *mridangam*, flute, *nadaswaram*, *kanjira*, *shehnai*, *santoor* violin, and *ghatam*. Sage Bharatha, the earliest Indian musicologist, is said to have lived in the first or second century CE. He founded Indian music on nine basic emotions or *rasas*: love, humor, pathos, anger, heroism, terror, disgust, wonder, and serenity.

The three-thousand-year-old music of India is today an art taught in infancy and requiring years of training. Indian music is written in scales. To the Western scale of twelve tones it adds ten microtones, making a scale of twenty-two quarter tones. Music notation is passed down by oral tradition from generation to generation. It is rarely written or read. It has no chords, but confines itself to undertones and a melody. It is not separated into bars. Melodies are unlimited and pursue endless improvisations and variations.

Each *raga* or theme consists of five, six, or seven notes, and the musician or singer constantly returns to this central kernel. Each raga has been invested with meaning and sacredness, suggesting a mood, color, personality, season, and time of day. There are several hundred ragas, and each raga is distinguished from the other in minute detail, capable of infinite improvisation. The *tal* or time cycle parallels the raga as it has a number of beats with significant differences.

Hindustani Music of Northern India

North India offers a wide range of forms of music, each with a specific history of development.

The *dhrupad*, developed during Akbar's sixteenth-century reign by Miyan Tansen and his master Swami Haridas, observes an antique stateliness and liturgical style. The *dhamar* lyrics are mostly based on the romantic episodes in the life of Lord Krishna and are supple and sensuous. The *khayal* is a combination of the dhrupad and the dhamar and is decorative and ornamented. The khayal proliferated into many *gharanas*, or schools. Each gharana has a specific style, tradition, and manner of rendition, and these styles are fiercely maintained. The Gwalior gharana is focused on linear transitions from note to note, a formal simplicity. The Agra gharana concentrates on dramatic contrasts and rhythmic syncopation, and the Rangeela gharana evolved with more lyrical warmth and color. The Khirana gharana prefers a slow tempo and is sweet and serene, while the Patiala gharana specializes in spectacular rhythmic play.

Carnatic Music of Southern India

In southern India, music reached a complex structure in the development of the *kriti*. Mostly devotional, it was molded to perfection during the first half of the nineteenth century by Shyama Sastri, Thyagaraja, Dikishtar, and Maharaja Swati Tirunal. The *pallavi* is the opening statement, in the lower and middle registers; the *anupallavi* is the elaboration in the middle and upper octaves, followed by *arabesques* over the whole range of registers with the pallavi being repeated like a refrain.

Musical Instruments

Most ancient musical instruments served to scare away wild animals, to communicate, to pray, and to entertain. Many old Indian flutes like the *nag phani* were shaped like snakes to tame dangerous serpents. The *leband-ti* from Tripupra, Assam, was shaped like a giant grasshopper to chase pests from the fields. The seals excavated from the Indus Valley civilization tell us about hourglass drums, castanets, cymbals, and clay whistles.

There are a great variety of instruments although only a few are used frequently. In the north, the bowed string is used for solo or accompaniment, the *sarangi*. The sitar and *sarod* (strings), the *shehnai* (reed), and the *tabla* or *pakhwaj* (percussion) are used predominantly in the north. In the south, the *veena* (strings), the *nadaswaram* (reed), and the *ghatam* and *mridangam* (percussion) are used in performances. Most Indian instruments have not changed over the years.

DANCE

Indian classical dance dates back to the first century CE. It is said that the sage Bharatha compiled the *Natya Shastra* or Treatise of Dance, which defined the six classical dance styles: Bharatanatyam, Odissi, Kathak, Kathakali, Mohiniattam, and Manipuri. Classical dances evolved in both sacred and secular spaces. Another dance is Kuchupudi, and Kalaripayattu is a martial art form of dance.

Bharatanatyam

Bharatanatyam is a form of classical dance originating in South India. Sculptural evidence from the fifth century BCE indicates the basic *araimandi* (half-sitting position) that is the form's basic posture even today. Bharatanatyam is believed to have had its origin from Bharat Muni, the author of the Natya Shastra (treatise on dance). In another story, it is said that the term is derived from the three words Bha (bhava, emotion), Ra (raga, melody), and Ta (tala, rhythm). It is essentially a solo dance and compositions of Carnatic music provide the repertory.

Bharatanatyam has two aspects: *nritta,* or the purely rhythmic, which is confined to footwork and movements of the body and hands; and *abhinaya,* or mime, which is conveyed through gestures and facial expressions.

Alarmel Valli, celebrated classical Indian dancer.

Odissi

Sculptural evidence of Odissi postures goes back to the second century BCE. From the twelfth century onward, inscriptions and manuscripts tell of ritual dances in temples. This dance was performed by *maharis* (female dancers) in the temple of Jagannath at Orissa, eastern India. Later, men also performed it in the courtyards of temples. In this dance the body takes the Tribhanga position, or thrice-deflected posture, in which the dancer's body is bent in three places approximating the shape of a helix. This posture and the characteristic shifting of the torso from side to side make Odissi the epitome of fluid grace, with a distinctive lyrical quality. Odissi is usually performed to the love lyrics of twelfth-century poet Jayadeva's *Gita Govinda,* which tells of the dalliance of Lord Krishna and his beloved Radha.

Kathak

According to legend, Kathak was performed by Lord Krishna with Radha and the *gopis* (cowgirls) by the banks of River Yamuna on the night of a full Moon. In ancient India, traditional storytellers (*kathakas*) performed the Krishna legend in temples. Later, when the Muslims invaded India, Kathak was performed by courtesans in secular spaces. In the early twentieth century, Kathak was revived as a serious classical dance form and later developed into two distinct schools called the Lucknow and Jaipur *gharana*. The influence of the Moghul rule and tradition is evident in the distinctive texture of the Kathak dance form as it evolved in northern India.

Characterized by a series of fluid pirouettes and rapid footwork echoed by the dancer's one hundred ankle bells, Kathak is an exciting display of beauty and dexterity. Its themes are taken from Persian and Urdu poetry, as well as Hindu mythology. Kathak evolved from the fusion of Hindu and Muslim cultures that took place during the Moghul period.

Kathakali

The distinctive dance drama of Kerala in southwest India, Kathakali literally means "play" in Malayalam. Several of the plays were written by kings and enjoyed royal patronage. As a compelling, dramatic dance form narrating incidents in mythology, it is three hundred years old but its origins go back much further. The dance and theater traditions in Kerala have merged and synthesized into an exacting discipline demanding at least twelve years of commitment, dedication, and training. Complete control of the body is required, from the eyebrows to the feet. A dancer must first shape his body with oil massage by the teacher's feet, training in the martial arts, gymnastic exercises, and a special diet.

A Kathakali performance includes dancers, actors, vocalists, and percussionists, and it lasts all night long. Traditionally performers are male and perform with no stage, backdrop, or scenery. The stage is defined by a temporary canopy of cloth hung on four poles. An oil lamp is lit to sanctify the space. Themes center around the slaying of an evil adversary. Each character has its own distinctive makeup, elaborate costume, and behavior. The makeup takes four hours to complete, with

Kathakali dancer.

the artists applying layers of rice paste in complex patterns. A tiny crushed seed is placed under each eyelid. The seed makes the whites of the eyes reddish, accentuating the character. An immense vocabulary of intricate hand gestures and eyes is used to express emotions, supported by percussionists and brass cymbals. Two onstage vocalists sing the entire text including narration and dialogue, which is characterized by repetition.

Mohiniattam

The dance of the celestial enchantress Mohini is graceful with exquisite fluid gestures. Mohiniattam became a distinct repertoire under the reign of Maharaja Swati Tirunal in the nineteenth century. Dancers wear a simple white or off-white costume with a red and gold brocade border.

A fascinating legend is associated with this traditional dance form. Brahma tells the other Gods how to obtain *amrit* the celestial ambrosia. (Amrit bestows immortality and power) He tells them that this can be achieved by churning the ocean of milk. As this is a daunting task the Gods ask the help of the demons. But the demons plot to keep the amrit for themselves. Lord Vishnu finds out the plot and and knows it would be catastrophic for the world if the amrit were to fall into the hands of the demons. So Lord Vishnu takes on the form of a celestial nymph/dancer/apsara and by way of his charms distracts them. The amrit is obtained by the Gods and the world is saved from the demons.

Manipuri

Manipuri is a lyrical dance form from the eastern region of India. Purely religious in content, the dance usually relates to the *Ras Lila*, the love story of Radha and Krishna. Manipuri is quite different from Odissi and Bharatanatyam. The knees are relaxed, and the body is turned into an imaginary figure eight. Unlike in Bharatanatyam, there are no sharp angles or straight lines. The fingers move in circles, semicircles, and curves. The form is placid, lyrical, subtle, and reminiscent of Balinese and Thai dances.

Kuchupudi

This classical dance form is from Andhra Pradesh. Kuchupudi is the name of a village in Divi Taluq in Krishna District. The dance was presented to the ruler Golconda King Hasan Tanesha. So impressed was the Muslim king that he gave about six hundred acres of land as an endowment to the Kuchupudi Brahmins. In the past, a Kuchupudi performance began the dancer hidden behind a moving curtain, over which her braided plait was thrown. She offers a challenge to any artist in the audience to compete with and surpass the performer of the evening.

Kalaripayattu

This impressive, ritualistic dance/martial art evolved out of combat practice exercises imparting suppleness to the muscles. *Kalari* is the school or gymnasium, a roofed pit of earth, and *payyatu* is exercise.

Martial arts evolved in the second and third centuries CE and are associated with herbal medicine. The reigning kings of Kerala supported many warriors who were experts in Kalaripayattu and who fought for their feuding kings. The guru, or instructor, is trained in the martial arts and also in medicine. Boys and girls begin training at eight years of age. Over the years they learn to wield and control various weapons and wooden rods, progressing through spears, shields, swords, and daggers and culminating in a six-foot sword with a sharp edge. They are prepared for their vocation by medicinal body massage.

Adjunct to the practice of Kalaripayattu is the clinical therapy Marma Chikitsa, knowledge of how to use the body's one hundred eight vital points to cure all ills, including disease and injuries. The practice also places a strong emphasis on mental discipline, focus, yoga, breathing techniques, and meditation.

Mythology connects Kalaripayattu to the teachings of the patron God of Kerala, Parashurama. Buddhist monks traveling on remote, inaccessible roads needed a method of self-defense, and historical evidence shows that this art was taught at the Shaolin temple in Tibet. The monks carried it throughout Asia, imbibing regional practices and developing it into varied styles of kung fu, karate, and tai chi.

～ 17 ～
Food: The Spice Route

*A*tithidevo bhava: "A guest is equal to God." This Sanskrit saying expresses the belief that a guest, whether visiting a hut or a palace, must be welcomed. In any Indian household food is always offered to anyone who enters. A housewife always cooks for an extra person in case someone comes visiting. When you enter a house, the first thing you are given is water. The host serves the guest first. When the meal is over, the host bids farewell to the guest with these words, "Go and return." There is no single word for goodbye in any of the Indian languages.

In India, food defines ritual, community, and kinship. The kitchen is a sanctuary, and images of deities are placed there for daily worship. Dishes and flavors vary from region to region due to the influence of the landscape, traditions, and religion. Each state has a distinct cultural identity and cuisine. Subtle or powerful Indian cuisine entices, tantalizes, and leaves an indelible memory of sensation and flavors. Surprisingly, the rice, wheat, barley, lentils, and fruits that the people of the Indus Valley civilization ate in 5000 BCE are still relished in India today.

Certain foods are regarded as sacred and are cooked for specific temple rituals and festivals. Each God is believed to relish one special dish, and during the celebration of the deity, the delicacies preferred by that particular God are cooked and eaten. Ganesh, the elephant-headed God has a sweet "tusk" for sugary dumplings made of rice flour, while *vadai mala*, garlands of *vadais* (crisp lentil cutlets) are made for Lord Hanuman, and any milk product is offered to Krishna, the God who often stole buttermilk and curds (yogurt) from his mother's kitchen. In the temple, a large kitchen prepares food for the Gods that is then distributed to the worshippers. At the holy shrine of Tirupathi in Andhra Pradesh, thousands of *laddus* (sweet dishes) are made for the pilgrims daily. In the temple of Jagannath at Orissa, one thousand people are employed in a kitchen with eight hundred stoves to cook for the deity.

Feast days, fast days, weddings, births, religious festivals, and other celebrations are occasions for food preparation. Food offers a personal experience and a link with tradition, in both its preparation and consumption. To create the perfectly balanced meal, one must include the six traditional tastes: spicy, sour, salty, bitter, astringent, and sweet. Ingredients are added to a dish not only because of flavor but for their medicinal qualities. Many Hindus abstain from foods thought to inhibit physical and spiritual development. Devout Hindus avoid garlic and onions, while dairy products are considered pure and are eaten to cleanse the body and mind. Many fast on specific days associated with a particular God or during certain lunar phases.

North Indian cuisine is known for its rich, hearty, and nutritious meals. Round cornmeal breads loaded with clarified butter (*makki ki roti*), or *parathas* (bread made from wheat flour) are eaten with shallow fried, fresh mustard greens (*sarson ka saag*) cooked in butter and ginger. A lentil dish (*dum aloo*) consists of tiny potatoes smothered in ground spices and roasted. Fresh cucumbers, tomatoes, onions, and radishes are diced with a dash of lime to enhance the zest of the meal.

In a Kashmiri home, breads resemble fine flaky pastry or bagels and are often dipped in steaming, subtly flavored tea. Breads like *naan* can be made in a clay oven fired by charcoal. Minced meat on skewers (*sheekh kabab*) or chicken pieces skewered and cooked in the clay oven are delicious. Tandoori chicken is baked whole in the oven. Lamb chops or kababs also are very popular, complementing the fresh cheese in a spicy spinach puree (*palak paneer*).

In the Bengal region of East India, fish is a specialty and can be broiled, curried, baked, or simply fried. Bengali sweets are perhaps the best in India. At a wedding feast, one might find thirty different sweet dishes. The best known is the *rasagolla,* spongy white balls of cheese boiled in sugar syrup. Pistachios, saffron, jaggery, and rosewater add to the color and taste of sweet dishes.

In West India, most of the people in Gujarat are vegetarians, and a typical meal might consist of rice, wheat bread (*roti*), salad, vegetable curry, yogurt, lentils, and pickles, along with a sweet dish. Gujaratis also indulge in deep-fried snacks of fried or steamed rice flour (*dhokla*), as well as dried fruits and nuts.

Goa near Mumbai (Bombay) has retained the Portuguese culture, and it influences the local cuisine. A Goan lunch would include fried chicken in a green masala paste, fish simmered in coconut milk with ginger and cumin, prawn soup, roast beef topped with a black cake made of jaggery rice flour, and coconut cream (*dodol*). And who can resist *bebinca,* a dessert made with forty eggs, butter, and coconut milk? On special days, pork is the featured dish. *Sarpotel*, a pork curry dish rich in spices, or roast suckling pig is consumed with gusto, aided by music and dancing.

Hyderabad in Andhra Pradesh is famous for *nahari*, a slow-simmered shank stew flavored with cardamom, which may include dried rose petals and other exotic spices. Keralites have their *pootu*, which is parboiled rice crushed with raw rice and mixed with grated coconut. This is stuffed into the hollow of a bamboo stalk and steamed.

Rice turns up in a variety of forms in South India. You could start off with a prepared rice breakfast, followed by rice for lunch, and the evening meal would again be served with a rice preparation. The dessert just might happen to be a rice pudding. There are many kinds of rice, ranging from the basmati (queen of fragrance) to sticky rice from Assam, red grains in Kerala, and the long grain rice in Bihar. Rice is a symbol of fertility and plenty. When a Hindu bride steps over the threshold of her husband's home, she tips a small container of rice into the house. The larger the area over which the rice is spread, the greater the good fortune that will enter the house.

South India is famous for its *iddli* and *dosa*. *Iddlis* are spongy steamed cakes made of lentils and rice flour, garnished with an array of pickles and chutneys. Low in calories and highly nutritious, they are the staple breakfast item in many homes. They can be dipped in lentil curries (*sambar*), coconut chutney, or spicy curry powder. Made from many ingredients, dosa comes in many forms. Rice and lentils are soaked, ground, and fermented. The next day, the batter is poured over a sizzling pan, drizzled with oil, and turned over after a minute. It is served with lentil curry or chutneys. Other dosas include Mysore dosa, pessarettu dosa, rava dosa, butter dosa, and paper dosa (two feet long). Coffee is served as well to round out the meal. It is filtered and made from beans roasted and pounded at home.

Nonvegetarian cuisine in South India comes from the Chettiars community in Chettinad. Dishes include spicy meatballs in a tangy sauce (*kola kozhambu*) and Chettinad fried chicken, which is known for its red chilies, curry leaves, onions, and a medley of spices.

Andhra, Assam, Karnataka, Madhya Pradesh, Uttar Pradesh, and many other states that embrace different creeds, communities, and traditions have their own fascinating perspectives on food.

In all of India, no meal is complete without the *paan*. It is a sweet, spicy, fragrant concoction of betel nut, lime paste, cloves, aniseed, cardamom, and fennel seeds, wrapped in an emerald green betel leaf. What do you do with it? Chew it slowly. It acts as a mouth freshener and a digestive.

Curry is synonymous with India. But the word "curry" may have originated from *karhi,* meaning wide vessel for making food. The word was probably anglicized during the British rule and became a generic term to describe any stew that included spices and gravy.

Sixty-three spices are produced in India. The oldest literary record of Indian spices is found in the Vedas: the Rig-Veda mentions mustard, the Yajur Veda makes reference to black pepper, and the Atharva Veda includes turmeric. There are references in Valmiki's *Ramayana* to King Dasaratha's body being preserved in spice oils and balms. Today, every Indian household prides itself on having on hand at least twenty fresh spices and spice blends. Specific blends are closely guarded family secrets.

India produces 2.2 million tons of spices annually. Pepper and cardamom are believed to have originated in the Western Ghats, while South India produces cardamom, ginger, turmeric, and pepper. Ginger is produced in most states, and chili is cultivated in Andhra Pradesh, Maharashtra, Orissa, West Bengal, Rajasthan, and South India. The most important seed spices, are coriander, cumin, fennel, fenugreek, celery, and dill seed. Saffron, the costliest spice, is cultivated mostly in Jamuu and Kashmir.

Spices are fragrant and can be used whole, ground, or in liquid form. Although most spices are used for seasoning and flavoring food, some spices like turmeric are used to improve the texture and introduce color to the food. The blending of spices is the essence of Indian cookery. *Masala* means a mixture of spices. There are hundreds of *masalas* from different regions imparting a distinctive flavor to each dish.

Here is a list of some common spices used in an Indian household.

AJWAIN
Gives food aroma and taste and is used for dal preparations, as well as meat dishes. Even the Ajwain leaves can be dipped in batter and fried. Resembles thyme. Good for upset stomachs and reduces acidity.

ASOFOETIDA
A digestive. It is always put into dried beans and split peas. A resin with an acrid bitter taste.

ANISEED
Has a sweet, delicate aromatic taste and can be used in dips, soups, seafood dishes, and salads as well as in meat dishes. It is

a mouth freshener and eliminates bad breath. Usually offered to guests after a meal or when they leave.

BAY LEAF
Used in rice dishes such as *pulaos* and *biryanis* (rice with meat, saffron, and spices like cloves, cinnamon, and cardamom). Boiled with water, it is a good antiseptic. It freshens the breath and is good for gums and eyesight. Is claimed to be an aphrodisiac.

CARDAMOM
Grown primarily in Kerala, Karnataka, and Tamil Nadu. It is used in sweet dishes and is an important ingredient of *garam masala* (mixed spices). Adds aroma and can also be used in pulaos and biryanis. Good for bad breath and used in tea.

CHILI
Used in all traditional curries, whole, ground or powdered. Dry red chilies are used as part of pickling, and the pungency varies and enhances the spiciness. Rich in vitamins A and C, green chilies are indispensable to Indian cooking.

CINNAMON
Taken from the inner bark of cinnamon trees, this has a mild, aromatic flavor. It is used in garam masalas and is ground or used whole for rice and meat dishes or stews and fish preparations. In stick form it can be used in beverages, and for pickling vegetables and chutneys. It is good for digestion.

CLOVES
This spice is the unopened flower bud of the clove tree, picked green and sundried. Used in whole and powdered form, it is

often fried with bay leaves, cinnamon, and cardamom for use in meat curries and stews. Cloves are often sprinkled over hot dishes before serving. Clove oil is used in the pharmaceutical industry as an antiseptic.

CORIANDER

Fresh green coriander is the base of most green curries and can be used as garnish to most dishes. It is also one of the main ingredients for all curry powders. It can be used for dips, salads, sauces, and pickles. It has a slightly lemony flavor.

CUMIN

Imparts warm flavors when roasted and powdered for meat or vegetable dishes. The seeds also are used in *sambars* and *rasams* and are fried in hot oil and poured over *dal* (boiled lentils) to improve the aroma. Good for broken capillaries and has a cooling effect.

CURRY LEAF

The leaves give flavor and are fried with mustard seeds and chopped onion. This is poured over the dish. Used in vegetarian dishes in the south.

FENNEL

A herb used in a wide range of curry powders, as well as seafood soups and salads. Used as mouth freshener.

FENUGREEK

The dried ripe fruit of an herb used in fish and vegetable dishes.

GARLIC

The bulb flavors all meals and is used to make chutneys and pickles. Pods of whole garlic also can be cooked and used in dips, salads, and chips. It stimulates blood circulation and reduces obesity.

GINGER

Cultivated in Asia for three thousand years. One of the oldest known spices, it is used extensively in Indian cuisine. Finely chopped, thinly sliced, or ground, it appears in chutneys and pickles. Used in squashes and rubbed over meats to enhance the flavor.

MUSTARD

Black mustard is used as a sharp flavoring agent and preservative. It prevents the growth of microbes. It is often fried in hot oil with curry leaves and chopped onion. The whole mixture is poured over curry dishes.

PEPPER

One of the most popular spices, black pepper is used in all Indian cuisine. Ground or sometimes used whole and can be found in meat and vegetable dishes. Good for blood circulation and is an astringent.

SAFFRON

The most expensive spice, it is bright yellow-red in color with a powerful aroma and an exotic, slightly bitter taste. Gives color to sweet dishes or meat preparations.

TAMARIND

The dried black pods of the tamarind tree are sour in taste and sticky. Good for flavoring lentils.

TUMERIC

The root of a plant, this is an essential spice and an important ingredient in all curries. Improves color and flavor. It is a preservative and can be used as a marinade for fish or added to pickles. As both an internal and external antiseptic, it makes the skin glow and purifies the blood.

Bibliography

Aditi: The Living Arts of India. Washington, D.C.: Smithsonian Institution Press, 1985.

Arnett, Robert. *India Unveiled.* Columbus, G.A.: Atman Press, 1996.

Ayyar, P. V. Jagadisa. *South Indian Festivities.* Calcutta: Rupa & Co., 1998.

Dalrymple, William. *The Age of Kali: Indian Travels and Encounters.* Victoria, Australia: Lonely Planet Publications, 1998.

Das, R. K. *Temples of Tamilnad.* Bombay: Bharatiya Vidya Bhavan, 1964.

Dowson, John. *A Classical Dictionary of Hindu Mythology and Religion.* Delhi: Rupa & Co., 1982.

Durant, Will. *Our Oriental Heritage: The Story of Civilization, Part 1.* New York: Simon & Schuster, 1954.

Gandhi, Mahatma. *An Autobiography: The Story of My Experiments with Truth.* Trans. Mahadev Desai. Boston: Beacon Press, 1957.

Goetz, Hermann. *India: Five Thousand Years of Indian Art.* Baden Baden, Germany: Greystone Press, 1959.

Hawley, John Stratton, with Goswami Shrivatsa, eds. and trans. *At Play with Krishna.* Princeton, N.J.: Princeton University Press, 1981.

Kundra, D. N., and S. D. Kundra. *History of India.* Delhi: Navdeep Publications, 1988.

O'Reilly, James, and Larry Habegger, comps. and eds. *Traveler's Tales: India.* Sebastopol, C.A.: O'Reilly & Associates, Inc., 1995.

Paz, Octavio. *In Light of India.* Trans. Eliot Weinberger. New York: Harcourt Brace & Company, 1997.

Punja, Shobita. "India Through the Ages." *The International Indian.* 7.6 (1999):12.

Renou, Louis, ed. *Hinduism.* New York: George Braziller, 1961.

Smith, Vincent A. *The Oxford Student's History of India.* London: Oxford University Press, 1908.

Spear, Percival. *A History of India,* Vol. 2. London: Penguin Books, 1966.

Tammita-Delgoda, Sinharaja. *A Traveller's History of India.* New York: Interlink Books, 1995.

Thapar, Romila. *A History of India,* Vol. 1. London: Penguin Books, 1965.

Watson, Francis. *A Concise History of India.* Norwich, Great Britain: Charles Scribner & Sons, 1979.

Wolpert, Stanley. *India.* Rev. ed. Berkeley: University of California Press, 1999.

Index

Note: Pages in *italics* indicate illustrations